AEI LEGISLATIVE ANALYSES
Balanced analyses of current proposals before the Congress, prepared with the help of specialists in law, economics, and government

Proposals to Regulate State and Local Taxation of Multijurisdictional Corporations

1981

97th Congress
1st Session

AMERICAN ENTERPRISE INSTITUTE
FOR PUBLIC POLICY RESEARCH
Washington and London

ISBN 0-8447-0241-2
Legislative Analysis No. 26, 97th Congress
August 1981

Contents

1

Introduction

Federal, state, and local taxation of businesses can have a significant impact on business incentive and decision making. Congress is currently reviewing the weight of federal taxes on business to determine the extent to which these taxes should be lessened to reduce barriers to business activity.

A related concern is the burden and fairness of state and local business taxes, which account for a higher and higher proportion of the taxes on business. Business firms have challenged these taxes on grounds that the activities taxed did not have a sufficient factual connection with the taxing jurisdiction, or that the tax was not fairly related to the services provided by the state or local government, or that the tax unfairly penalized activities in interstate or foreign commerce, or that the tax was not fairly apportioned to local activities.

In passing on the validity of state and local business taxes, the Supreme Court has given state and local jurisdictions the benefit of the doubt, noting that it is not the appropriate body to devise standards to regulate such taxation. Rather, the Court has pointedly stated that the power granted to Congress under the commerce clause of the U.S. Constitution would amply justify the enactment of federal legislation establishing standards governing the taxation of business activities that are not exclusively local and requiring these bodies to adhere to uniform rules—for example, for the division of income among the various jurisdictions.[1] This legislative analysis will examine legislative proposals to regulate state and local taxation of business firms and review the arguments that are advanced in favor of, and in opposition to, these proposals.

2

Background

The thrust of the proposed legislation discussed in this analysis is directed primarily at state and local imposition of income taxes, sales and use taxes, and gross receipts taxes on business firms. This section will discuss the taxation of multistate and multinational corporations, particularly as it relates to those three types of taxes. It will review states' efforts to achieve greater uniformity among themselves and thus discourage the enactment of federal legislation mandating greater uniformity. It will also review prior efforts to enact federal legislation regulating such taxation and discuss provisions of international tax treaties that have been proposed to ameliorate certain tax problems.

Status of Existing Law

The power to tax is inherent in state sovereignty. In fact, state and local governments are not even prevented from levying oppressive taxes, unless such taxes contravene specific provisions of the U.S. Constitution. State franchise or license taxes for the privilege of conducting a strictly interstate business within a state were held invalid for many years.[2] When a business had activities and property both within and outside a state, the Supreme Court, in the leading case of *Western Union Telegraph Company* v. *Kansas*, concluded that the state could not require the company to pay a tax on property permanently located outside the state as a condition for conducting an intrastate business as well.[3] A state's assessment of a permit or franchise tax based on the par value of all of a multistate corporation's capital stock, according to the Court, directly burdened interstate commerce in contravention of the commerce clause; and the application of the tax to property beyond the geographical confines of the state and not subject to its jurisdiction constituted an unconstitutional taking of property without due process of law, contrary to the Fourteenth Amendment.[4]

In *Norfolk & Western Railroad* v. *Missouri Tax Commission*, the tax commission determined the total value of the railroad's rolling stock and allocated a portion of that value to the state of Missouri based on track mileage within the state as a percentage of the railroad's total track mileage. The railroad showed that the allocated value greatly exceeded the value of its rolling stock within the state, either on the date of the assessment or on average. The Court concluded that the state could not, by the use of an imprecise allocation formula, validly extend its taxing authority beyond its borders.[5]

Despite cases like these, however, the Court has given state and local authorities wide latitude in fashioning taxes to suit their needs, and it has repeatedly noted that Congress is the body to which requests for more precise regulation of the taxation of multistate and multinational corporations should be addressed.

Income Taxes. All but six states levy a general corporate income tax at marginal or flat rates that range from 4 to 12 percent. Corporate income taxes account for 9.7 percent of all state tax collections, aside from unemployment taxes. Sixteen cities with populations of 125,000 or more also levy corporate income taxes ranging from 1 to 9.5 percent. Only five states permit the deduction of federal income taxes in arriving at net corporate income subject to state tax. One state permits deduction of half of the federal income tax paid or accrued during the taxable year.[6]

As noted above, a state cannot give its tax laws extraterritorial effect.[7] Thus, when a corporation operates in more than one state or in more than one country, a state that wishes to tax the corporation must determine a proper allocation of the corporation's income to its activities within that state. One way in which a state may accomplish this is by the separate accounting method. That is, the accounts of units and subsidiaries of the corporation within the state are examined to determine the income and expenses of each. The value of products and services transferred from one corporate unit or subsidiary to another, including out-of-state units and subsidiaries, at other than fair market value, is recomputed as if the entities were dealing with each other at arm's length. A corporation's business operations within the state are treated separately and distinctly from its business outside the state, and net income for income tax purposes is computed as if the corporation's activities were confined solely to that state.[8]

The federal government also uses the separate accounting method for income tax purposes. Although the federal government is not concerned with the allocation of income among states, it is concerned with allocating income between the United States and the foreign countries in which the tax-paying corporation and its affiliated firms operate.[9]

Most states use an apportionment formula employing factors relevant to the production of income—usually property, payroll, and sales—to determine in-state and out-of-state income. Many of these states have extended the formula apportionment approach by adopting a "unitary method" of accounting that includes the incomes of all related corporations that are part of a "unitary group." State definitions of a unitary group variously refer to related corporations in a corporate family (including those outside the taxing state) that are linked together in a single stream of business, or that are dependent upon or contribute to the business of the corporation within the taxing state, or that have centralized management and are operated as one unit. Some scholars would limit the unitary group concept to situations in which the property and activities within the taxing jurisdiction are an *inseparable* part of the business carried on both within and outside the jurisdiction.[10] The rationale for classifying numerous firms as part of a unitary group is that the group's operations form a single integrated business and the group's activities should be treated the same whether accomplished through a single entity or through use of a number of firms.

Twenty-six states employ the unitary approach in taxing the income of multistate corporations and their affiliated firms, and a growing number of states (eight in 1980) employ the unitary approach in taxing multinational corporations and their affiliated firms.[11] The unitary approach treats each member of an affiliated group engaged in the same line of business as part of a single enterprise. Thus, no income is realized until there is a sale to, or other transaction with, an unrelated firm or party. Losses sustained by one affiliate are offset by the profits of other affiliates. Under the unitary approach, the taxable income includes the aggregate incomes of all affiliated firms in the unitary business. (Some related firms, of course, do not engage in the same unitary business—for example, Mobil Oil Corporation and Montgomery Ward & Company.) The net aggregate income for all affiliated firms, less the deductions permitted, is then apportioned as outlined below to avoid extraterritorial taxation. Most states that employ the unitary approach use an equally weighted three-factor formula to allocate income from a unitary operation. This is accomplished by dividing the total sales, payroll, and tangible property of the unitary business by the average ratio of sales, payroll, and tangible property in the taxing state. If, for example, one-fourth of the sales, payroll, and property factors are within the taxing state, one-fourth of the aggregate income of the unitary group is apportioned to that state for income tax purposes. A state may also elect to employ an equally weighted two-factor formula, or it may give added weight to one factor in a three-factor formula, or (as in Iowa) the state may rely on only one factor in apportioning income.[12]

Different results may be obtained by states that employ the equally weighted three-factor formula as a result of differing definitions of tangible property or the other factors. Furthermore, some states allocate sales to the state of destination, while others allocate them to the state in which the sale originated. Some states exclude certain types of income, such as earnings from real property, capital assets, or interest and dividends, in arriving at net income, but an increasing number treat all income as business income.

Eight states have extended the unitary approach to worldwide groups that include foreign as well as U.S. corporations, thus employing worldwide combination accounting to reach all income of the group. If more than one member of the group is subject to tax within a state, the tax liability is divided between them in relation to the applicable factors. Variations in apportionment formulas among the states, the differing weights given by each state to income factors, differing definitions of income, and varying descriptions of what constitutes a unitary group permit the states to determine for themselves how much of a group's national or worldwide income is subject to tax. States lack the direct power to tax extraterritorial income, however, and taxpaying corporations periodically ask the Supreme Court to strike down provisions of state income tax laws which the corporations believe apportion an excessive share of income to the state. The states employing such apportionment formulas invariably claim that they are not taxing extraterritorial income. They claim that they are using apportionment formulas as a sourcing technique to determine what is, and what is not, in-state income.

The federal government has the power to tax extraterritorial income and does so, even though a number of other industrialized nations do not. Foreign income derived from related corporations, however, is generally not taxed by the federal government until it is repatriated or returned to this country, for example, as a dividend paid by a foreign subsidiary to a U.S. parent corporation. Even then, firms subject to federal income taxes are allowed to take (subject to some limitations) a dollar-for-dollar tax credit to offset the income taxes that they pay to foreign governments, to avoid multiple taxation.

In the 1959 case of *Northwestern States Portland Cement Company* v. *Minnesota*, the Supreme Court sought to clear away the underbrush of past decisions concerning the power of the states to tax interstate commerce.[13] The Court concluded that, absent the exercise of Congress's exclusive power to regulate such taxation under the commerce clause of the U.S. Constitution, the states could apportion the entire net income of a national corporation generated by interstate as well as intrastate activities, if that income was fairly apportioned among the states. According to the Court, the founders of the nation did not intend to immunize interstate commerce from paying its fair share of the cost of a state government in return for the benefits it derived within a state.

In *Moorman Manufacturing Co.* v. *Bair*, decided in 1978, the Court upheld the single-factor tax formula used by Iowa in the apportionment of income between in-state and out-of-state activities, even though a majority of the Court acknowledged that use of a single-factor formula, when most of the states employed a three-factor formula, created a risk of duplicative taxation.[14] But until Congress prescribed a different rule, the Court stated, business firms that objected to the single-factor formula would have to prove that the formula produced arbitrary results. Four of the nine justices dissented. In the recent case of *Exxon Corporation* v. *Wisconsin Department of Revenue*, Exxon relied on separate accounting for three activities (marketing, exploration and production, and refining) to dispute the state's assertion of a right to tax Exxon's Wisconsin activities (marketing functions that operated at a loss) on an apportioned basis of Exxon's overall income from all operations.[15] Exxon read the Court's *Moorman* decision as sanctioning the use of separate accounting to show that income apportioned to the taxing state was in fact earned in another jurisdiction.[16]

The Court reviewed its prior pronouncements, including the requirement that the plaintiff bear the burden of showing extraterritorial taxation by "clear and cogent" evidence, and concluded that Wisconsin was not bound to recognize the company's separate accounting and that more than a *risk* of multiple taxation must be shown. Thus, absent legislative action by Congress, the unitary approach can be applied to the taxation of the income of multistate and multinational corporations and their affiliates, and a showing of actual multiple taxation will be required to prove that a state's use of the unitary approach offends the Constitution.

Taxation of Intercorporate Dividends. The federal government generally does not tax dividend income from foreign sources until it is repatriated and does not tax a foreign subsidiary as it earns income outside the United States.[17] Federal income tax law allows domestic firms to deduct from their taxable income 85 percent of the dividends received from another domestic corporation and 100 percent of the dividends received from a domestic subsidiary. This is done because the income from which the dividends are paid has already been taxed by the federal government. No deduction is allowed for dividends received from a foreign corporation not engaged in business in the United States, but duplication of income taxes is avoided by allowing a foreign tax credit for income taxes paid to a foreign government.

Seventeen states follow the federal rule on the deduction of dividends received from a domestic subsidiary, and seven exempt such dividends from taxes. Three states allow a deduction based on different ownership percentages than are provided for by federal tax law. The deductions do not depend on whether the earnings of the subsidiary distributed as dividends have previously been taxed by either the taxing state or any other state. The remaining states tax dividends from domestic corporations at a higher rate than the federal government, but only five states provide no deduction at all.[18]

Twenty-seven states tax intercorporate dividends received from subsidiaries abroad, and seventeen tax dividends that are "deemed paid" for the purpose of calculating taxes but that are not actually distributed to the in-state corporation. A few states allocate dividends entirely to the state where the U.S. firm is domiciled, and some states exempt dividends received from foreign sources from taxation.[19]

In the case of *Mobil Oil Corp.* v. *Commissioner of Taxes of Vermont,*

Mobil carried on a wholesale and retail petroleum marketing business in Vermont. Vermont used an apportionment formula to tax a portion of Mobil's dividend income from foreign sources, even though Mobil's principal place of business and corporate domicile were in New York.[20] Mobil contended that there was no nexus, or connection, between its wholesale and retail merchandizing of oil products in Vermont and its management of foreign investments through its commercial domicile in New York or the business activities of the foreign corporations paying the dividends. It argued, moreover, that New York was entitled to tax the dividends fully and that this, and the risk of multiple taxation at the international level (a major share of its dividends were from firms incorporated abroad and either wholly or partially owned by Mobil), justified the exclusion of dividend income from apportionment by Vermont.

The Court, however, concluded that a sufficient connection was shown because Mobil availed itself of the privilege of carrying on business in Vermont. In other words, it refused to accord the state of domicile the exclusive authority to include foreign dividend income in the corporation's tax base. Instead, it approved of treating foreign dividend income as part of the stream of income accruing to a unitary business and thus apportionable to Vermont. Justice John Paul Stevens filed a vigorous dissent, arguing that Mobil's investment income, which was far greater than its operating income, had no special connection with the company's operations in Vermont and that the investment income was improperly lumped into Mobil's tax base in Vermont. Moreover, Stevens maintained that the sales, payroll, and property values that were connected with the production of the dividend income, for the firms paying dividends to Mobil, should be added to the denominator of Vermont's apportionment formula. Otherwise, he said, the formula would overstate Mobil's taxable income by as much as tenfold.[21]

By refusing, for the most part, to allow a tax credit to offset taxes paid by subsidiary firms out-of-state or abroad, and by taxing unrepatriated as well as repatriated earnings, the states have stimulated demands for federal legislation to limit state taxation of intercorporate dividends.

Sales and Use Taxes. A high percentage of state and local governments require in-state business firms to collect sales taxes from consumers. Many states also impose the burden of collecting a use tax (generally, a tax on the privilege of using personal property that has come to rest in the state) on out-of-state sellers because of the impracticality of trying to collect the sales tax from in-state consumers on sales originating outside the state. Because use taxes compensate for revenues that would be lost because of the difficulty of collecting a sales tax in such cases, they are sometimes referred to as compensating use taxes.[22] Reported tax revenues from general sales taxes normally include use tax revenues as well. General sales taxes account for 31.6 percent of all tax revenues raised by the states, exclusive of employment taxes, and selective sales and gross receipts taxes account for another 15.3 percent. Some 5,460 local jurisdictions also levy general sales taxes that account for 8.8 percent of their total tax revenues. Another 4.4 percent of their revenues are raised through special sales and gross receipts taxes.[23]

In *Scripto* v. *Carson* the Supreme Court sustained the liability of an out-of-state seller for a state use tax.[24] Sales were made within the taxing state of Florida by ten "independent contractors" who worked on a commission basis and forwarded orders to an out-of-state seller for acceptance and collection. This was held to provide a sufficient connection with the state to defeat the argument that the tax was an impermissible burden on interstate commerce and violated the due process clause. In *National Bellas Hess* v. *Illinois*, however, the seller had no office within or franchise from the taxing state, and it advertised and delivered its products solely through the mails or by common carrier.[25] In that case the Court held that there was not a sufficient nexus with the taxing state and noted that if Illinois could impose liability for the use tax on an out-of-state mail order house, every state, municipality, school district, and other political subdivision could do likewise. The Court said that "the many variations in rates of tax, in allowable exemptions, and in administrative and recordkeeping requirements could entangle National's interstate business in a virtual welter of complicated obligations to local jurisdictions with no legitimate claim to impose 'a fair share of its cost of the local government,' " when the purpose of the commerce clause was to ensure a national economy free from such local entanglements.[26]

In the more recent case of *National Geographic* v. *California Equalization Board*, however, the Court found a sufficient nexus to sustain the state's requirement that an out-of-state mail order seller of magazines collect and remit the use tax.[27] The *National Geographic* maintained two offices in California to solicit advertising copy, and in the Court's view this was sufficient connection, even though sales of the magazine and related products were handled entirely by mail.

A good deal of uncertainty persists, notwithstanding the Court's opinions. Out-of-state sellers are faced with a confusing array of state taxes, and the states, fearing the unwarranted loss of tax revenues, demand the remittance of taxes upon the slightest indication of a sufficient nexus with the seller to impose tax liability.[28]

Gross Receipts Taxes. A small number of states and other governmental bodies have either gross receipts taxes or franchise taxes whose amount is measured by a firm's gross receipts from sales in the taxing jurisdiction. Many scholars consider a tax based on gross receipts to be inequitable, since a firm may have to pay a significant amount of taxes even though it is operating at a substantial loss. As in the case of use taxes, the authority to impose a gross receipts tax on an out-of-state firm depends on the extent of the firm's connection with the taxing jurisdiction. In *Norton Co.* v. *Department of Revenue of the State of Illinois,* the Supreme Court said that it was easier for a state to show that a transaction was subject to its sales or use tax laws than to establish the circumstances giving rise to liability for the franchise tax. Cases involving sales or use taxes were not controlling in cases involving a franchise tax measured by gross receipts because the latter tax falls on the seller.[29] In the *Norton* case the seller obtained state consent to do business in Illinois, and it operated a branch office and warehouse in the state from which it made local retail sales, sales admittedly covered by the state's tax law. The tax statute, however, specifically exempted business firms in interstate commerce from the tax. The Court noted that the seller could have made sales through solicitors only and thus have been tax-exempt, but that it could not channel business through the local outlet and still obtain the immunity granted to an interstate business. The Court did hold, however, that gross receipts from orders sent directly from purchasers to the out-of-state seller and filled by direct shipment to the purchaser were so clearly interstate in character as to be exempt from the franchise tax.

In the 1975 case of *Standard Pressed Steel* v. *State of Washington Department of Revenue,* however, the Court took a narrower view of the protection afforded out-of-state sellers by the commerce clause.[30] In that case the seller had no office in the taxing state, but it did have a full-time salaried employee who worked out of his home ascertaining the needs of the seller's principal customer and dealing with difficulties encountered by the customer in using the seller's products. The presence of the employee was held sufficient to uphold the state's tax on the unapportioned gross receipts of the seller from sales in the state. The Court acknowledged the risk of multiple taxation from a gross receipts tax, but it ruled that the seller had not demonstrated actual duplicate taxation.[31] The breadth of the Court's ruling in *Standard Pressed Steel* has stimulated business support for legislation to establish a standard similar to that employed in *Norton*.

Prior General Federal Legislation

The 1959 *Northwestern States* case and related decisions of the Supreme Court led to demands that Congress provide greater clarity regarding the circumstances under which the states can tax net income derived from interstate commerce. Congress was asked to establish jurisdictional standards defining the activities a business firm could undertake without incurring income tax liability. Congress then enacted Public Law 86–272, approved on September 14, 1959, prohibiting states and local governments from imposing a net income tax on out-of-state firms if their operations within the taxing jurisdiction were confined to certain minimal activities, which were specified in the statute. Under the new law, a firm not incorporated under the laws of the state would not be subject to a net income tax if its only activity was the solicitation by an employee of orders for tangible personal property that were sent out of state for approval or rejection and filled by shipment or delivery from a point outside the state. An out-of-state firm would also avoid taxation if its missionary sales people solicited orders for a wholesaler or other dealer who in turn sent its orders outside the state for approval or rejection and whose orders were filled by shipment or delivery from a point outside the state. Business firms were also exempted from state income tax if the solicitation of orders was handled by independent contractors with or without an office in the state if their only activity was the making of sales or the solicitation of orders for sales.[32]

A number of courts have construed the 1959 statute narrowly and have sustained the imposition of state income taxes when the activities specified in the law were augmented by other activities or by the presence of company property in the state. Examples of such additional activities have included the rental of property and a salesman's performance of consulting or repair services.[33] But other courts have characterized such additional activities as incidental to the solicitation of sales and have thus given the statute broader application.[34]

Public Law 86–272 does not preclude the imposition of sales and use taxes or gross receipts taxes on out-of-state firms, and pressure for jurisdictional standards for state and local taxes of these kinds has continued.

Prior Proposals for Federal Action

Public Law 86–272 was the first significant legislative reaction to calls for a federal statute to provide greater uniformity in state tax treatment of multistate businesses. Five years later, in 1964, the Special Subcommittee on State Taxation of Interstate Commerce of the House Committee on the Judiciary (the Willis subcommittee) issued a report alleging major defects in the system of state and local taxation of businesses engaged in interstate and international commerce.[35] The report noted that the states, as a result of favorable judicial decisions, were broadening the scope of business tax obligations. The result, according to the report, was a pattern of state and local taxation that could not be made to operate efficiently and equitably when applied to companies that operated in many states. The report recommended restrictions on state income, capital stock, gross receipts, sales, and use taxes imposed on interstate commerce. The subcommittee also recommended that tax policy affecting companies that operate either wholly or partially outside the United States should be set by the federal government and not by the individual states. Whether income from sources outside the United States could be included in income subject to state apportionment should depend, according to the subcommittee, on whether that income was taxable by the federal government.

Representative Edwin E. Willis (D-La.), the subcommittee chairman, introduced a comprehensive bill to deal with various problems in the taxation of multistate and multinational firms in 1965, but the bill ran into a storm of criticism from the states and from business firms. The Multistate Tax Compact referred to in the section on "State Efforts to Achieve Greater Uniformity" was proposed in 1965 as an alternative to federal legislative efforts. Thereafter a modified bill was introduced by Representative Willis in 1966 as a result of reaction to the first bill. After additional modifications had been made in this draft, it was introduced in 1967 by Representative Willis. This bill passed the House, as modified in committee, but did not receive Senate attention.[36] The Multistate Tax Compact became effective in August 1967, following ratification by seven states.

A bill similar to Willis's 1967 bill was introduced by Representative Peter W. Rodino (D-N.J.) in 1969; this bill also passed the House but failed to receive attention in the Senate.[37] Similar bills have been introduced in each succeeding Congress through the 96th Congress. A bill introduced by Senator Warren G. Magnuson (D-Wash.) in the 92d Congress represented the work of state tax administrators and business representatives who sought to effect a compromise by allowing the Multistate Tax Commission (discussed in the section on "State Efforts to Achieve Greater Uniformity") to arbitrate disputes, but the commission itself did not support these efforts.[38]

In 1973 the Senate Finance Committee established a Subcommittee on State Taxation of Interstate Commerce. Senator Walter F. Mondale (D-Minn.), who chaired hearings by this subcommittee, cited the almost total lack of agreement between the states and business interests as the reason why Congress had not enacted legislation and recommended additional attempts to reach agreement.[39] Further negotiations were held in 1974 and 1975, but the resulting compromise draft did not receive substantial support from either the states or the business community, and there have been no significant negotiations since then.

During hearings in Congress in 1975 on tax reform legislation, a witness for the Council of State Chambers of Commerce suggested the addition of a provision to exclude income from foreign sources from state income taxation. Representative James B. Jones (D-Okla.) proposed an amendment to effect this change, but the chairman of the Ways and Means Committee, Representative Al Ullman (D-Oreg.), succeeded in having the matter referred to the Task Force on Foreign Source Income chaired by Representative Dan Rostenkowski (D-Ill.). In 1976 a witness for the same organization suggested that the tax reform bill under consideration by the Senate be amended to restrict state taxation of that portion of international investment income that, under the Internal Revenue Code, was allocated to sources outside the United States, and that the states not be permitted to use worldwide combination accounting for apportioning income from foreign sources as defined in the Internal Revenue Code.[40]

Representative Rostenkowski's Task Force on Foreign Source Income filed its report in March 1977. In it, the task force recommended that the states be precluded from taking into account the income of foreign affiliates of firms doing business within the states until such time as that income was subject to federal income tax.[41] The states could then apply a three-factor apportionment formula. Senator Herman E. Talmadge (D-Ga.) proposed that the task force recommendations be adopted as an amendment to the tax reform bill, but the markup of the bill was concluded without consideration of the Talmadge proposal. Although three members of the task force had jointly introduced legislation to carry out the task force recommendations, their bill received no attention, and Senate action on the tax provisions of the United Kingdom tax treaty received priority in the following Congress.

In 1977 Senator Charles McC. Mathias (R-Md.) introduced S. 2173 to provide for federal judicial review of the application of jurisdictional guidelines for state taxation of interstate commerce and for the apportionment of interstate income among the states, and he presided over extensive hearings on that bill for the Senate Judiciary Committee. In May 1978, Chairman Ullman of the House Ways and Means Committee asked the General Accounting Office (GAO) to conduct a study of the methods employed by the states in taxing multinational corporations, and that report is expected to be issued shortly.

Bills were introduced in the 96th Congress (1979–1980) to foster commerce among the states by providing a system for the taxation of interstate commerce, and bills to limit the taxation of income from foreign sources were also introduced as S. 1688 and H.R. 5076, and hearings were held on these two bills.[42] A modified version of S. 1688 and H.R. 5076 has been introduced in the 97th Congress, and the bills incorporating this version will be discussed in the chapter "Features of Principal Legislative Proposals," together with S. 983 of the 96th Congress, which will be reintroduced in the 97th Congress. We are advised, as this is written, that the replacement for S. 983 will be the same as that bill in most respects.

State Efforts to Achieve Greater Uniformity

The Uniform Division of Income for Tax Purposes Act (UDITPA). In 1957 the National Conference of Commissioners on Uniform State Laws, as a part of its ongoing effort to achieve greater uniformity in state legislation, proposed a Uniform Division of Income for Tax Purposes Act (UDITPA). State legislatures are free to adopt or to ignore such proposals, or to adopt them with modifications. The UDITPA proposal deals with the allocation or apportionment of income of taxpayers having income from business activities both within and outside a state adopting the uniform law (state A for ready reference). If other states claiming a sufficient nexus to tax a firm's income do not adopt the uniform statute or interpret it differently, of course, the goal of uniformity is defeated. Section 3 of UDITPA acknowledges the right of a state other than state A to apportion and tax business income if the firm is subject to a net income tax, a franchise tax, or a corporate stock tax in that state, but, if the second state follows ground rules that differ from those used by state A in determining jurisdiction to tax, the benefits of substantial uniformity may be lost.

The provisions of UDITPA that would assist in achieving greater uniformity if the act were universally adopted and construed consistently from state to state include the following. All business income, defined as income from transactions and activity in the regular course of a firm's trade or business, would be apportioned among the states. States that adopted UDITPA without modification would employ an equally weighted three-factor formula, consisting of payroll, sales, and the average value of the taxpayer's real and tangible personal property owned or rented during the tax period, to allocate business income.[43]

Nonbusiness income would be allocated to a specific state rather than apportioned among several states. Such income would be allocated to the state where the property producing the income was located, to the state in which the property was utilized, or to the state where the company had its commercial domicile according to the detailed rules spelled out in UDITPA.[44]

The Multistate Tax Compact. Following the Supreme Court's decision in the *Northwestern States* case in 1959 and the congressional activity that followed, some states became concerned that Congress might adopt legislation restricting their authority to tax firms engaged in interstate and foreign commerce.[45] To counter this possibility, representatives of the National Association of Tax Administrators, the National Association of Attorneys General, and the National Legislative Council, working under the auspices of the Council of State Governments, drafted a proposed multistate tax compact in 1966. Article IV of that proposed compact incorporated the proposed Uniform Division of Income for Tax Purposes Act. Thus, if the compact was universally adopted and if UDITPA was construed in the same manner in all states, uniform rules for the allocation of nonbusiness income would be assured. Business income, a more limited concept than that employed by numerous states, would be apportioned among the states under a uniform allocation formula, with uniform definitions of relevant terms. Hence, the risk of duplicative taxation would be reduced. Seven states had ratified the compact by 1967, thus, by its own terms, rendering it effective as a compact. Until the adoption of the compact, very few states had enacted

UDITPA. In 1978, in *U.S. Steel Corporation* v. *Multistate Tax Commission*, the Supreme Court rejected a challenge to the compact's constitutionality.[46]

Article VII of the compact authorizes the Multistate Tax Commission, created in article VI and composed of tax administrators from the member states, to adopt uniform advisory regulations. The commission's regulations depart from UDITPA by, in effect, eliminating the distinction between business and nonbusiness income, thus making almost all income subject to apportionment.[47] Article VIII authorizes the commission to perform an audit of a firm or firms at the request of any member state or local government of such a state (joint audits for two or more states are sometimes performed), and the commission as auditing agent may seek compulsory process. Member states, however, retain complete control over all legislative and administrative actions affecting their tax rate, the composition of their tax base, the means and methods of determining tax liability, and the collection of any taxes due. The commission has also established advisory regulations, forms, and guidelines on matters to which UDITPA does not apply.

States may withdraw from the Multistate Tax Compact, and some states have done so. Currently, the Multistate Tax Commission has nineteen member states who fund the commission through dues payments based on their tax revenues. Associate members, of which there are eleven, may attend commission meetings, but they do not pay dues nor do they participate in most of the commission's activities.[48]

The Tax Treaty Approach

Treaties ratified by the U.S. Senate have the force and effect of law to the extent that their provisions are self-executing, as is true of most tax treaties. Thus, one solution to some of the problems arising from state and local taxation of multinational corporations would be a series of bilateral treaties with other nations that would effectively limit or override state and local laws. The model tax treaty employed by U.S. negotiators is patterned after the model treaty of the Organization for Economic Cooperation and Development. Adoption of the model is viewed by the Department of the Treasury as offering the best chance for achieving the maximum degree of international tax harmonization and the reduction of tax-based barriers to the free movement of goods and capital across national borders, with appropriate protection against both double taxation and tax evasion. The purpose of a tax treaty is not to eliminate taxation but to allocate the authority to tax income that might otherwise be taxed by more than one government.[49] Dan Throop Smith, former deputy to the secretary of the Treasury for tax policy, has pointed out that tax treaties establish common rules on the allocation of income. Each country usually allows a credit for the income taxes paid in the other country in order to avoid double taxation.

The concept of a "permanent establishment" is also recognized through treaties, so that each country taxes a foreign company only if it maintains a permanent establishment in the taxing country. This permits a firm to engage in casual and exploratory commercial contracts in another country without being subject to its tax laws.[50]

The U.S. tax treaty negotiated with the United Kingdom illustrates one approach to dealing with state taxation of firms with foreign parents or affiliates. Under paragraph 4 of article 9 of the treaty as initially proposed, a state or political subdivision could not combine the income of the U.S. branch of a British corporation or any related foreign enterprises with that of the British corporation in determining the income of the U.S. branch. Alternatively, if a British corporation did not do business in the state but had a U.S. subsidiary doing business there, the state could not require combined reporting that includes the income, payroll, or property of the British parent or other related foreign enterprises.[51] Of course, the United Kingdom and its political subdivisions would be similarly constrained with respect to U.S. corporations and U.S. subsidiaries. However, a protocol of reservation excluded the application of paragraph 4 of article 9 to subnational governments on the grounds that restricting state taxing practices objected to by the United Kingdom should be considered by both houses of Congress rather than just the Senate and that the relevant congressional committees would consider federal legislation restricting state taxing practices.[52]

More recently, the U.S. tax treaty with Canada omitted a similar provision desired by Canada, but with the understanding that Canada regards unitary apportionment with combined reporting as resulting in inequitable taxation and imposing excessive administrative burdens on Canadian companies doing business in the United States. If an acceptable provision on this issue can be devised, the United States will reopen discussions with Canada on this subject.[53]

The tax treaty approach to limiting state and local taxation of multinational corporations can be resorted to if the full Congress does not have to deal with the issues involved. The treaty approach, however, does not reach the problems involved in state and local taxation of domestic multistate operations. In addition, it would be cumbersome, for it would require a separate, identical treaty with nearly every nation in the world.

3

Features of Principal Legislative Proposals

This analysis will discuss three recent bills introduced in Congress to deal with state and local taxation of multistate and multinational firms. They include S. 983, originally introduced in the 96th Congress and slated to be reintroduced in the 97th by Senator Mathias; H.R. 1983, already introduced in the 97th Congress by Representatives Conable, James R. Jones, Bill Archer (R-Tex.), Bill Frenzel (R-Minn.), and James G. Martin (R-N.C.); and S. 655, introduced in the 97th Congress by Senators Mathias, Lloyd M. Bentsen (D-Tex.), and Walter D. Huddleston (D-Ky.). The terms of these bills will be discussed in conjunction with particular types of state and local taxes and as they would affect litigation over state and local tax liability.

Net Income Taxes

S. 983 does not attempt to distinguish business income from nonbusiness income. Rather, taxing jurisdictions would be free to establish their own definitions and to apply or not apply the unitary principle and combined reporting in taxing corporations that are taxable in more than one state, subject to an overall limit on the tax base set by provisions of the bill.[54] Thus, the tax could not exceed the tax that would be derived by employing an equally weighted three-factor formula encompassing property, payroll, and sales factors applied to the tax base as that base is restricted by other provisions of the bill.[55]

The following additional ground rules would apply in arriving at the bill's limitation on the tax base. Income from foreign sources and dividends from corporations in which the taxpaying corporation owned 50 percent or more of the voting stock would not be apportioned to or allocable to any state. (For the taxation of income from foreign sources, see the subsection "Income from Foreign Sources.") Dividends (other than dividends from foreign sources) received from corporations in which the taxpaying firm owned less than 50 percent of the voting stock would be allocable to the state of commercial domicile and not apportionable or allocable to any other state. The taxing state could require, or the taxpaying corporation could elect, combined reporting of the income of all affiliated corporations[56] except for income from excluded firms enumerated in note 54 and income from corporations 80 percent or more of whose gross income was derived from sources outside the United States in the current taxable year and in each of the two preceding taxable years. Individual states and corporations also could agree to consolidate income in a manner at variance with the ground rules set in the bill.

Multistate and multinational corporations would continue to compute their income tax liability as provided under state law. The proposed federal ground rules for determining the tax base would only be resorted to if their use yielded a lower tax liability than that provided by state law. Even then, state law would continue to apply except as specifically overridden by the terms of S. 983. The bill is designed to prevent too much or too little of a corporation's income from being assigned to a particular state.

Income from Foreign Sources

S. 983 defines foreign income to include interest, dividends, rents, royalties, and license and technical fees from property located or services performed "without the United States," and gains, profits, or other income from the sale of intangible or real property located "without the United States." The term "United States" is defined as the fifty states and the District of Columbia. Thus, income from Puerto Rico and the territories and possessions of the United States would be income from foreign sources, and it would not be included in the federal ceiling on the state and local income tax base. Similarly, worldwide combination accounting would be prohibited for domestic and foreign corporations substantially all of whose income was derived from sources outside the United States and for the types of corporations enumerated in note 54.

H.R. 1983 and S. 655 are essentially identical. These bills would prohibit states from including the income of foreign corporations or foreign affiliates of American corporations in the income tax base of a corporation doing business in the states through application of the unitary method on a worldwide combination basis or otherwise until that income became subject to federal income tax, that is, generally, when it was repatriated. The corporation doing business in the states would usually be a corporation organized under the laws of one of the states, but it could also be a U.S. branch of a foreign corporation. Certain corporations organized under U.S. law would be treated as foreign corporations for the purposes of this clause. A domestic corporation would be treated as a foreign corporation, for example, if less than 20 percent of its gross income for the preceding three years was from sources within the United States.

Another part of these two bills deals with restrictions on state and local taxation of dividends received by corporations from foreign sources. While S. 983 would exclude interest, rents, royalties, license and technical fees, and gains or profits in setting a tax base ceiling, H.R. 1983 and S. 655 would limit state taxation of foreign dividends but not other income from foreign sources. In practical effect, these bills would allow a corporation receiving a dividend from a foreign corporation a tax credit (comparable to that provided by federal law) applicable against state and local income taxation of that dividend to offset the foreign income taxes paid on the dividend by the U.S. corporation and the foreign income taxes paid by the foreign subsidiary attributable to the earnings distributed in the dividend. If the foreign tax rate exceeded 46 percent (the current marginal federal tax rate on corporations), the dividends from the foreign source would be completely exempt from taxation by state and local governments. If the foreign tax rate was less than 46 percent, a proportionate part of the dividend would be exempt. Thus, if the foreign tax rate were 23 percent (half of the current U.S. rate of 46 percent) the state could not tax more than half of the dividend. This exclusion would permit the states to tax, at whatever rate they apply to other income, only that portion of a dividend from a foreign source that the federal government effectively taxes after taking into account the foreign tax credit.[57]

Imposition and Collection of Sales and Use Taxes

S. 983 would codify federal jurisdictional ground rules for state and local taxation of interstate sales of tangible personal property and the circumstances in which out-of-state sellers could be required to collect a use tax on such sales. These ground rules have been proposed as a way to reduce double taxation and to ease the burden of complying with state and local sales and use tax laws, particularly for smaller sellers. An interstate sale would be treated as consummated in the state to which the property was shipped or delivered. A state or subdivision of a state could not impose a sales tax on the interstate sale of tangible personal property occurring outside the taxing jurisdiction unless the taxing jurisdiction had a cooperative agreement with the destination jurisdiction and the firm had a business location in the taxing state. Even though a taxing jurisdiction has the authority to assess a sales or use tax on an interstate sale, it could not require the interstate seller to collect and remit the tax unless the seller had certain minimum connections with the jurisdiction, namely, a business location in the taxing jurisdiction, or regular solicitation of orders in that jurisdiction by representatives in that jurisdiction, or regular delivery of tangible personal property in that jurisdiction by means other than common carrier or the U.S. Postal Service.[58] A business location within the state would be deemed to exist if the firm owned or leased real property within the state or had an employee located in the state (compare Public Law 86–272 as to income taxes) or regularly maintained a stock of tangible personal property (other than goods for consignment sale) within the state for sale in the ordinary course of its business. An employee within a state would have to be an employee within the meaning of the federal income tax withholding provisions and one who performed significant services within the state, or one who performed significant services in that and other states but had a single principal place of business within that state. If the employee did not have a business location within the state, he or she would not be considered to be located within the state if sales orders were sent outside the state for approval or rejection and orders were filled by shipment from outside the state. This would also be true for an employee who only performed installation or repair services that were incidental to interstate sales of property. S. 983 would also prohibit the inclusion of transportation charges on tangible personal property in the tax base for an interstate sale if such charges were separately stated by the seller.

S. 983 includes several provisions specifically designed to ease the burdens imposed on smaller sellers in interstate commerce who are faced with a maze of reporting and tax requirements from political subdivisions that impose sales and use taxes. A taxing jurisdiction could not require an out-of-state seller to collect its sales or use taxes if the seller's annual receipts from sales of property with a destination in that state were less than $20,000. The seller would not be liable for the collection or payment of the sales or use tax on any transaction for which the purchaser furnished a certificate or written statement either that the purchaser was exempt from the tax or that it had registered with the taxing jurisdiction to pay the tax. Under a buyer certification plan for an out-of-state seller who had made less than $100,000 of sales in a particular state the previous year, the seller could elect to accept the buyer's certified statement as to the proper combined amount of state and local sales or use taxes to be collected on a transaction and the seller's obligation to collect the tax would be satisfied by collecting that amount, unless the seller had actual knowledge that the certificate was false or inaccurate. The secretary of commerce would prescribe standard reporting forms for sellers reporting collections based on the purchaser's certification. All taxing jurisdictions would be required to accept this form, and the seller's certification would not have to be submitted more often than quarterly. No seller would be required to classify interstate sales according to geographic area within a state except for subdivisions in which the seller had a business location or regularly made deliveries other than by common carrier or the U.S. Postal Service. Provisions for the allowance of credit and for refunds are included in the bill to avoid duplicate payment of taxes on the same tangible personal property.

Jurisdiction to Impose a Gross Receipts Tax

S. 983 would overrule the Supreme Court's *Standard Pressed Steel* decision by restricting state and local authority to impose a gross receipts tax on interstate sales of tangible personal property to situations in which the sale was solicited through a business office of the seller in the taxing jurisdiction; that is, the seller would have to own or lease real property in the jurisdiction or regularly maintain a stock of tangible personal property in the taxing jurisdiction (other than on consignment) for sale in the ordinary course of business. This amendment would bring the required nexus between the seller and the taxing jurisdiction closer to the status recognized in the Court's earlier decision in *Norton*.

Federal Court Review

S. 983 would permit either the corporation or the taxing jurisdiction to appeal an adverse determination as to any issues arising under the terms of the bill or under Public Law 86–272 governing nexus for purposes of imposing state and local income taxes. This appeal would lie to the U.S. Court of Claims within ninety days after the decision of the relevant administrative body within the state. The factual findings of the administrative body would be considered by the Court of Claims, but the proposed legislation does not give these findings any special weight or presumption of correctness. The Court of Claims would try the case anew and not on the administrative record. The decision of the Court of Claims would be binding on the state if it was a party to the court proceedings or if it was given notice of the court's decision. No statute of limitations would bar recovery of the amount of the court's judgment if action was taken to recover that amount within one year after the court's determination became final.

4

Issues and Arguments

Fairness

The pending legislative proposals make no attempt to regulate the types of taxes imposed by state and local governments or the tax rates that might be applied by the taxing jurisdictions. Their practical effect would be, as far as income taxes are concerned, to regulate the tax base employed by states and localities when taxing firms engaged in interstate and foreign commerce. This section discusses the fairness of existing state and local tax practices and the unfairness of the pending bills, as viewed by opponents, and the fairness or unfairness of revenue losses to state and local governments.

Views of the Legislation's Proponents on State Income Taxes. S. 983 would invoke the regulatory powers of Congress under the commerce clause of the United States Constitution to compel greater uniformity of income-tax base treatment among state and local jurisdictions. Proponents of the bill contend that this would eliminate many distortions in the tax treatment of corporations engaged in interstate and foreign commerce, eliminate taxation of the same income by more than one jurisdiction, and thus foster greater fairness.

State collections of corporate income taxes amounted to about 5 percent of federal corporate income taxes in 1950, but they amounted to more than 18 percent of such federal taxes in 1980.[59] The states' increased reliance on corporate income taxes clearly intensifies the importance of this form of taxation to the taxing authorities, to those taxed, and to those who might be taxed were it not for the sums collected from corporations. The fairness of state-to-state taxation of corporate income commands increasing attention as states rely more heavily on the corporate income tax and as cities and other local governments increasingly utilize this revenue-raising measure. State and local income taxes affect many multistate firms. Although multinational firms are less numerous, they claim that the most serious abuses of state and local tax authority involve them.

Proponents of the pending proposals make the following specific arguments:

S. 983 would eliminate most of the distortions in the allocation of income from state to state. Advocates of this proposal maintain that combined reporting of income and differing apportionment formulas and ground rules for taxation among the states produce serious distortions in the allocation of corporate income to the states and may allocate more than 100 percent of a firm's income to the states. Double taxation of the same income, advocates claim, is more prevalent than the proposed legislation's critics and the courts have been willing to admit.[60] Some states, it is asserted, have refused to adjust their apportionment factors even when distortions have been pointed out to them. In some cases states have required combined accounting when it was to their advantage but not when it was to the advantage of the taxpaying corporation.[61] A state with little industrial development may double-weight the sales factor of the apportionment formula or use a single-factor formula based on sales, while a state with heavy industrial development may double-weight the property or payroll factors or employ only these two factors in the formula. Advocates of the legislation say that, notwithstanding the refusal of the Supreme Court to condemn Iowa's single-factor formula, the dissent of Justice Lewis F. Powell, Jr., clearly showed that differences in state apportionment formulas do produce double taxation. Justice Powell maintained that Iowa allocated to itself as taxable income all of the income derived from interstate sales completed in Iowa. Nonetheless, other states taxed some portion of the same income through the property and payroll factors in their three-factor formulas, and thus these taxes produced double taxation.[62]

Proponents maintain that S. 983 would eliminate many of the distortions in the allocation of income, since an equally weighted three-factor formula would be used and all taxing jurisdictions would use the same formula. There still could be some misallocation of income, however. One example would be where a firm that heavily invested in its home jurisdiction and received low profits on its operations there but earned good profits in other states. In such an instance the property factor in the apportionment formula might import income into the home jurisdiction. Advocates of S. 983 maintain, however, that the bill would go a long way toward eliminating the most serious distortions in the allocation of income.

Present tax practices adversely affect small businesses. Advocates of the proposed legislation claim that smaller corporations suffer most from excessive or duplicative taxation through the application of differing ground rules from state to state. The amount of extra taxes imposed on them may not be large enough to justify their making large expenditures on attorneys' fees and litigation costs to challenge the assessments. Larger corporations, on the other hand, often make a practice of contesting tax assessments and are able to obtain relief from the most egregious tax rulings.

Differing ground rules, aside from apportionment formulas, adversely affect multistate businesses. The states employ differing definitions and principles in the application of their tax laws that also produce instances of unfairness, distortion, and double taxation, according to proponents of the proposed law. States differ, for example, in determining which income is subject to apportionment among several states and which income should be assigned to a single state. Using an apportionment formula to allocate nonbusiness income causes such income to be assigned in whole or in part, according to some advocates of the legislation, to states having little or no connection with the assets or activities that produced the income. Thus, when the state of commercial domicile, for example, fully taxes this same income, the result is double taxation. The gain from a sale of timber land in Mississippi was fully taxed in that state, according to one company witness, when timber was not relevant to the company's current product line. Six other states then apportioned that income in a way that produced an additional $500,000 in tax revenues for them.[63]

Worldwide combination accounting produces serious inequities. Proponents maintain that even if all of the states used the same apportionment formula and identical definitions in their tax laws, there would still be serious misapportionment of income if foreign operations were included through worldwide combination accounting. As a British industry representative pointed out, "California and other states have continually broadened the concept of 'unitary business' in the last thirty years, with the result that affiliated corporations all over the United States and the world have become increasingly subjected to the indirect long-arm bookkeeping requirements and tax gathering mechanism predicated on the unitary business concept."[64] Critics of this trend also maintain that the unitary concept has been extended to encompass unrelated lines of business of sister corporations in other countries, a practice that is unfair because stockholders of the domestic corporations are taxed on profits which they may never share.[65]

Advocates of the proposed legislation maintain that apportioning income from the worldwide operations of affiliated corporations produces the most extreme examples of unfair taxation. They support the traditional tenet that a state must earn its tax revenues by providing some kind of protection or service for the income-producing activities and naturally cannot do so for the overseas operations of affiliated corporations. Aside from the unfairness of taxing such foreign income, advocates say, worldwide combined accounting may produce distortions because the operating circumstances of affiliated firms overseas may be vastly different from those of domestic firms, and accurate translation of the various factors into American dollars may be impossible. Accrual accounting may be required in one country, while cash accounting rules obtain in another. Different levels of inflation and rapid currency fluctuations may produce still other distortions. Labor costs may be substantially lower in foreign countries, meaning that high property and sales factors for firms operating in the United States will allocate a disproportionate amount of income to state and local jurisdictions. Combination accounting fails to recognize that a higher rate of return is required in countries like Iran and Nicaragua to offset the much higher risks of doing business there. Worldwide combination accounting assumes that businesses earn the same rate of return on each dollar of property, payroll, and sales, but, according to the advocates of federal legislation, this assumption is erroneous, particularly when foreign operations are included in combined reporting.[66]

Advocates of the legislation cite examples of the distortions caused by the application of worldwide combination accounting. The deputy director of the California Department of Economics and Business Development, for example, acknowledged that corporations can lose money on their business operations in California and still owe a substantial income tax to the state. The Sony Corporation added TV picture tube production at its color TV assembly plant in San Diego, and the resulting increase in the property and employment factors produced an increase in Sony's California income taxes even though Sony's earnings in California declined. ALCAN Aluminum Corporation had a loss on its U.S. operations, but with worldwide combination accounting California computed a tax liability of $229,000 for the firm. In another case, a multinational corporation acquired a company operating exclusively in California, a company whose operations were losing money and were totally different and substantially smaller than those of the parent corporation. Yet California's use of worldwide combination accounting was reported to have apportioned 50 percent more of the multinational's profits to the state. Anderson, Clayton & Company had no federal taxable income from U.S. sources in 1969, but by employing worldwide combination accounting California assessed $71,000 in taxes against the company.[67]

Advocates of the legislation maintain that the unitary business concept with worldwide combination accounting nearly always apportions more income to a taxing state in this country. They maintain that they are looking for a method that allocates the income of corporations engaged in interstate and foreign commerce to the appropriate states but does not allocate more than 100 percent of their income. In their view, worldwide combination accounting prevents uniformity, and the need for uniformity requires the enactment of federal legislation.[68]

Views of the Legislation's Opponents as to State Income Taxes. Critics of S. 983 maintain that the legislation would permit multistate and multinational corporations to avoid paying taxes on some income, would reduce the revenues of some taxing jurisdictions, and would substitute a federal standard for state and local concepts of fair taxation. It would entrench combined accounting domestically, favor some states over others, disadvantage small businesses, and limit the authority of state and local tax officials to set tax policy in accordance with their own notions of fairness.

S. 983 would entrench the principle of nationwide combination accounting. Opponents point out that while the cited bills would ban worldwide combination accounting, S. 983 would compel all states wishing to apportion domestic income to use nationwide combination accounting and the same apportionment formula. This, they contend, would entrench combined accounting in the fabric of our tax law, a practice that is roundly condemned by many proponents.

S. 983 would favor some states over others. Some opponents object to S. 983 on grounds that it would attribute all dividend income to the state of commercial domicile rather than permitting its apportionment among various states. A number of states oppose complete allocation of dividend income to the state of commercial domicile because this would favor states with substantial commercial activity, such as New York, over market states. In their view, marketing is the fuel of manufacturing and commercial activity, and market states should be allowed to apportion dividend income.[69]

The bills would prevent achieving full tax accountability. Opponents of the proposals contend that such legislation would open loopholes that would allow corporations to evade accountability for all their corporate income. S. 983, for example, in conjunction with the jurisdictional constraints of Public Law 86–272, would restrict jurisdictions from taxing income attributable to certain sales activities. The tax laws of many states, and section 16 of the Uniform Division of Income for Tax Purposes Act, permit the state from which a shipment of tangible personal property is made to claim the sale as a sale within that state if the sale is not taxable in the state of the purchaser. S. 983, on the other hand, contains no "throwback provision" that would enable a state to allocate to itself income from corporate sales that escaped inclusion in some other state's sales factor. This, opponents contend, is contrary to the objective of the states, which is to achieve 100 percent taxation of the relevant multistate activities of corporate taxpayers. They argue that S. 983 would permit large amounts of income, so-called nowhere income, to escape taxation.[70]

Opponents respond to the argument that the states may tax more than 100 percent of a corporation's income through the application of differing apportionment formulas by noting that such differences may also permit corporate income to *escape* taxation. Example 2 in table 1 provides an illustration of undertaxation due to differing apportionment formula provisions.

TABLE 1

THE EFFECT OF APPORTIONMENT OF INCOME OF CORPORATIONS AND AFFILIATES UNDER COMBINED REPORTING

	Example	Property Factor	Payroll Factor	Sales Factor	Net Income Apportioned to State per Average of Factors in Formula
1.	Each state applies an equally weighted three-factor formula.				
	State A:	55/90	20/30	20/90 = 135/270 =	50 percent
	State B:	35/90	10/30	70/90 = 135/270 =	50 percent
2.	State A applies an equally weighted two-factor formula.		20/30	20/90 = 80/180 =	44 percent (undertaxation if equally weighted three-factor formula is accepted as the norm)
3.	State B applies an equally weighted two-factor formula.		10/30	70/90 = 100/180 =	55 percent (overtaxation if equally weighted three-factor formula is accepted as the norm)

NOTE: This hypothetical example assumes income factors based on the following dollar totals (in millions of dollars) for each of two states in which the corporation and its affiliates operate:

	Property	Payroll	Sales
State A	55	20	20
State B	35	10	70
TOTALS	90	30	90

SOURCE: Author.

The bills would cause substantial revenue losses. The proposed bills, according to opponents, would have a serious adverse impact on the revenues of states and localities. In addition to the risk that some corporate income would escape taxation, as explained above, S. 983 would ban the taxation of any kind of income from foreign sources, while the other bills would restrict the taxation of dividends from foreign sources. Imposing a foreign tax credit provision on the states would, in practical effect, exclude most such income from state taxes because many foreign countries tax income at as high or at a higher rate than the federal government. S. 983 would also preclude the taxing of dividends from some domestic subsidiaries, dividends that are now taxed by some states and localities. Income from firms in which the taxpaying corporation owned less than 50 percent of the voting stock would be assigned to the state of the taxpaying corporation's commercial domicile and would not be apportionable to other states. This would cause a loss of revenues in states that would otherwise apportion these dividends. While such a step would prevent double taxation of dividends, opponents maintain that such income would escape taxation if the state of commercial domicile did not tax these dividends. Their view is that apportionment is preferable because it recognizes that many states contribute in fact to the economic welfare of the corporation, and apportionment accompanied by throwback provisions assures that 100 percent of a multistate corporation's activities will be subject to tax.[71]

Estimates of the revenue losses that would have occurred if S. 2173 (the predecessor of S. 983) had been enacted varied widely from state to state, depending on total corporate income per state, state and local tax law provisions, and the official making the estimates. The deputy attorney general for Florida testified that a change from Florida's income tax apportionment formula (which gives a 50 percent weight to sales) to an equally weighted three-factor formula would cost that state approximately 6 percent of its overall corporate tax revenues, or $11.6 million. The commissioner of the Indiana Department of Revenue estimated that the bill would cost his state at least $12 million in net income tax revenues ($10 million through loss of throwback of sales) and another $8 million in gross income taxes. The California State Franchise Tax Board estimated that it would lose $485 million in bank and corporate income taxes. Representatives of four other states provided estimates of overall tax losses but did not segregate losses due to changes affecting state income taxes alone.[72]

The bills would prevent state and local authorities from setting tax policy according to their own notions of fairness. Opponents of federal legislation, responding to proponents' claims of unfairness, ask, "Who is to say that a tax is all out of proportion to the benefits provided by the taxing jurisdiction?" They point out that the Supreme Court did not strike down state income taxes on this ground when minimum contacts with the taxing state were established. "Don't tell us how to run our affairs," states assert, "that's our decision." The distortions proponents claim are caused by state and local income tax laws that produce double taxation, according to opponents, have not been shown to be a serious problem. The Supreme Court has power to strike down laws that produce double taxation, but it has not done so. Even in the *Moorman* case—a case whose dissenting opinion is often cited by the proponents of federal legislation—a majority of the Court did not find an overlap of taxes sufficient to justify invalidating Iowa's apportionment formula. Proponents have also cited distortions due to differing state definitions of business income and of nonbusiness income, but opponents note that none of the cited bills would deal with this issue.

The bills would discriminate against intrastate firms and small businesses. Failure to force multistate and multinational corporations to "fully account" for income, according to opponents of federal legislation, would give them an unfair advantage over intrastate businesses, which cannot escape full accountability. Intrastate corporations, moreover, would continue to pay taxes on dividends received if the proposed legislation, which would exclude certain dividends from the tax base of corporations in interstate and foreign commerce, was enacted. It is also noted that multistate businesses could avoid some income taxes attributable to interstate sales because some part of their sales would be consummated in states in which there is insufficient nexus for the state to impose a tax and there is no throwback provision in S. 983 to permit capture of the income from these transactions by another state. Furthermore, multistate corporations could make sales in states that have no corporate income tax and here too there would be no throwback provision to permit another jurisdiction to capture those transactions in its apportionment formulas.[73] Intrastate businesses, it is argued, would not have the opportunity granted to multistate firms to achieve favorable tax results by attributing a major share of their profits to jurisdictions where lower corporate income tax rates prevail.[74]

Opponents also charge that if the pending bills were enacted they would primarily benefit extremely large corporations. The California State Franchise Tax Board claims that slightly more than 5 percent of all corporations would receive the major benefits of a bill like S. 983. These corporations earn 50 percent of the income reported in California. Another 11 percent of the corporations filing returns in California would receive some benefits, and these corporations earn 22 percent of the income reported in California. The remaining 84 percent of the corporations, with 28 percent of the income, presumably would be unable to escape full accountability.[75]

If the pending legislation is enacted, according to opponents, state and local jurisdictions will be forced to impose other taxes, raise corporate tax rates, or cut services at a time when the federal government is reducing its funding to the states. If corporate income tax rates are raised to offset lost revenues, according to opponents, smaller businesses in particular will suffer.

Proponents' Rejoinder. Advocates say that whether or not state and local governments raise tax rates to offset revenue losses from enactment of the federal legislation, intrastate and multijurisdictional corporations will share the income tax burden fairly, which is not the case now. They acknowledge that some state authorities have felt strongly that inclusion of sales in the apportionment formula would be very much in the interest of low-income states, while including property and payroll in the formula would favor high-income manufacturing states. In 1964, however, the Special Subcommittee on State Taxation of the House Judiciary Committee concluded that the states that do most of the producing also offer the biggest markets. Thus, according to the subcommittee, inclusion of the sales factor (or a more heavily weighted sales factor) may have some effect on the allocation of income tax revenues, but the effect is minor, considering the high administrative cost of assuring compliance.[76] Some advocates of the federal legislation also contend that the claim that some states will suffer a great loss of revenue from a federal ceiling based on an equally weighted three-factor allocation formula is erroneous, since these states are both market states and producer states.[77] In addition, proponents maintain that if replacing combined accounting with the arm's-length standard employed by the federal government would produce a substantial revenue loss, this confirms the proponents' belief that combined accounting and the allocation of income by formula result in unjustifiable extraterritorial taxation.[78] Thus, to the extent that this is true, S. 983 would only cause a loss of revenues that the states should not have collected in the first instance, and the bill would correct a situation that unfairly favors intrastate business and disadvantages multijurisdictional businesses.

Proponents of federal legislation also claim that throwback rules applied by some of the states should be dropped, as is proposed by S. 983, because they do not serve as an accurate measure of a corporation's business within the state benefiting from throwback and because application may thwart the deliberate choice of the state from which throwback is claimed, such as New York in the *Mobil* case, not to tax certain income-producing activities.[79]

Proponents of the law also say that the failure of the Supreme Court to find that nationwide or worldwide combined accounting and alternative apportionment formulas have resulted in such overlap of taxes as to violate the Constitution proves nothing, since the Court made it clear that it is not the appropriate body to work out rules for the allocation of taxable activities to the states and, consistent with this, it applies a very loose standard. The Supreme Court has acknowledged that "The freedom of the states to formulate independent policy in this area may have to yield to an overriding national interest in uniformity."[80]

Proponents also deny that the pending legislation would primarily benefit large corporations. They note that since smaller firms operating in interstate and foreign commerce lack the resources to contest tax assessments and thus have paid taxes they should not have paid, these smaller firms would benefit more proportionately than large firms. Some states might benefit from fairer tax burdens, since they could then attract firms that now avoid doing business in them because of these taxes.[81] (See additional arguments on this issue in "Effect on Commerce and Economic Efficiency.")

Views of Proponents on Taxes on Income from Foreign Sources. Proponents maintain that worldwide combination accounting and current state tax practices "import" income that should not be taxed because the states and localities have not earned the right to tax that income by providing services. They also contend that economic and foreign trade benefits would flow from enactment of the proposed legislation. More specifically, proponents make these arguments:

Worldwide combination accounting improperly imports income. The worldwide combination accounting method is unjust, it is claimed, when it includes the income of a foreign parent of a U.S. subsidiary and the foreign parent does no business in, and has no connection with, the taxing state. Senator Mathias has referred to worldwide combined accounting as a method by which the states "have stretched their apportionment nets to ensnare foreign source income."[82] This, according to some business spokesmen, is income the states have no right to tax. Overlapping and duplicative taxation is substantially more pronounced in the case of income from foreign sources, it is claimed, because there are greater disparities in wage rates, inflation rates, required investment, and so forth between operations in this country and operations abroad. Even if the states had the federal government's authority to tax extraterritorial income, it is asserted, they should allow a foreign tax credit, but most do not. Combined reporting, moreover, effectively taxes foreign income that the U.S. parent corporation has not yet received because it has not been repatriated. If the foreign country has blocked currencies, or even if it never does, the income that is taxed may never be repatriated.

International practice, apart from some countries that do not tax foreign source income at all, is to tax only income that has been repatriated. Some states, however, not only tax the income of foreign subsidiaries as it is earned but also tax part of that income a second time when it is paid to the U.S. parent.

The states have not earned the right to tax such income. Worldwide combination accounting and the use of the three-factor formula to allocate income are advocated by the opponents of federal legislation to obtain a rough approximation of the portion of a firm's income attributable to the state. But where dividends represent the income of another corporation earned by its activities completely outside the United States, according to advocates of the legislation, the U.S. corporation has made no contribution to earning the income and should not be taxed. Advocates note that if the corporations were unrelated and the U.S. firm bought products from the foreign firm and sold them in this country, the states could not tax the income of the foreign corporation. They do not see why the situation should be any different because the U.S. corporation owns stock in the foreign corporation.[83]

Taxing such income unfairly discriminates against foreign trade. Proponents point out that if foreign taxes are counted, dividend income may be taxed three times, aside from federal taxes. Bills to regulate state and local taxation of such income should be enacted, they claim, to reduce the disincentives that currently discourage repatriation of foreign income. In addition, proponents of federal legislation allege serious adverse economic, foreign trade, and international relations effects from state taxation of income from foreign sources. Business spokesmen feel S. 983 is preferable to H.R. 1983 and S. 655. The latter bills are regarded as a compromise proposed by certain members of Congress in an attempt to overcome the continuing stalemate over federal legislation. Many businesses, however, regard state taxation of dividends from a foreign source as the most egregious abuse that needs to be remedied. They believe it is important to resolve this dispute even if agreement cannot be reached on legislation to resolve the other policy questions.

Views of Opponents on Taxes on Income from Foreign Sources. Opponents contend that the states have earned the right to tax foreign source income and that firms would escape 100 percent taxation if this income were not taxed. Adoption of the legislative proposals, they say, would encourage intercorporate transfers to reduce corporate taxes. The specific points made by opponents of the legislation are as follows:

Worldwide combination accounting is necessary to cover 100 percent of corporate income. Opponents declare that the states are entitled to consider income from foreign sources in apportioning income for tax purposes for a corporation doing business in the state. Donald H. Clark, the commissioner of revenue for Indiana, has used the example of a hypothetical motion picture company that spends $20 million to produce a motion picture that grosses $20 million in the United States. The company also distributes the motion picture worldwide and takes in an additional $10 million abroad. Clark maintains: "If we don't tax foreign income in that case, they have gotten away with a third of the income as net, as opposed to writing off 100 percent of their costs against the United States income."[84] Ferdinand P. Schoettle, professor of law at the University of Minnesota, contends that if a firm produces oil in a foreign country through one subsidiary, ships it in a tanker owned by another subsidiary, refines it into gasoline in a refinery owned by another subsidiary, sells the gasoline at wholesale through another subsidiary, and sells the gasoline at retail through still another subsidiary, the taxing state should be able to treat the entire operation as a unitary business and tax the income as apportioned, for not all of the income was produced in the country of production or by the tanker company.[85] The state in such cases, according to opponents, does not tax foreign income. It merely apportions income under a formula that provides a rough approximation of the contributions that the taxing jurisdiction makes to the unitary business, all that is required under the decisions of the Supreme Court.[86]

As to the argument that differences in wage rates and other factors between the United States and foreign countries skew the apportionment of income in favor of taxing states in this country, the chief tax counsel for Oregon maintains that no one has made an empirical study of this issue and thus no one can determine the amount of income that should be allocated to the United States because of U.S. know-how, whether it is management, patents, or copyrights.[87]

Worldwide combination accounting prevents evasion of taxes through corporate manipulation. Opponents of the proposed legislation contend that worldwide combination accounting prevents the deliberate creation of separate corporate bodies and manipulation of their activities to minimize taxes owed to the states. Transactions among members of a corporate family can be the vehicle for the transfer of income from one corporation to another and from one taxing jurisdiction to another. The arm's-length method of adjusting the prices of intercorporate transactions is employed by federal tax authorities to adjust the accounts of members of corporate families. Opponents maintain that the bills would require the states to follow federal practice and thus segregate income from foreign sources. The arm's-length approach, it is claimed, is far from accurate and poses serious problems for the states in arriving at fixed fair-market prices for intercorporate transactions and determining whether expenses benefiting more than one corporation are fairly and equitably distributed.[88] Opponents of the legislation claim that tax liability under the unitary approach and worldwide combination depends on substance rather than on legal fictions and corporate shells, because the unitary method "washes out" transfer pricing, tax havens, and other tax avoidance techniques, thus placing multinational businesses on a more equal footing with intrastate firms.[89]

Opponents contend that U.S. corporations own nearly 30,000 foreign corporations. These foreign subsidiaries contributed $16.9 billion of net earnings to multinational operations, and dividends from foreign subsidiaries added approximately $5 billion to the income of U.S. corporations that pay federal, state, and local taxes.[90] Some opponents maintain that dividend income is like any other income and that it would be unrealistic to make any distinction as to tax treatment of that income. All income, it is argued, is derived to promote the pecuniary status of the corporation, and the fact that the corporation elects to receive income in one form rather than another should not alter the tax consequences. Dividend income, in this view, should be apportioned among the states like any other income. Otherwise, providing preferential treatment for dividend income will encourage U.S. corporations to repatriate more income in the form of dividends.

Harriet A. King, commissioner of the Vermont Department of Taxes and an opponent of the federal legislation, contends that federal income tax law, in allowing a credit for foreign taxes paid on income from foreign sources, is irrelevant to state taxation. The chief tax counsel of the Oregon Department of Justice has expressed fear that adoption of H.R. 1983 and S. 655 might mean a loss of $20 to $25 million in revenues for Oregon.[91]

The bills unfairly discriminate against unincorporated businesses. Opponents note that the bills only affect corporations. Thus, income from foreign sources paid to unincorporated businesses would continue to be taxed as before in a number of states, thereby favoring multinational firms and placing smaller businesses at a competitive disadvantage.

Proponents' Rejoinder to Opponents' Views on Sales and Use Taxes. Responding to criticism of the separate accounting approach and the arm's-length method of adjusting intercorporate transactions, proponents of federal legislation claim that pricing is based on the prices obtained for similar transactions between unrelated companies, that the Internal Revenue Service (IRS) is very aggressive in its administration of the arm's-length approach, and that the states can rely on the work done by the IRS to reduce their own auditing. They claim that the unitary principle is based on three assumptions that are not valid, particularly when applied to multinational operations, that the assumptions underlying the separate accounting method have greater validity, and that in any event the transactions between related domestic and foreign corporations are not nearly so numerous or varied as those between related companies in this country. The separate accounting method determines the profitability of separate corporations separately, whereas the unitary approach assumes that the separate profitability of related corporations cannot be determined. Proponents of the legislation also maintain that American businesses do not establish separate corporations abroad to avoid taxes but rather to develop business that would not otherwise be available.[92] In addition, the advocates claim that some states apply the unitary principle when there is insufficient basis in the operations of the related corporations for doing so.

Views of the Proponents on Ground Rules for Sales and Use Taxes. Advocates contend that most interstate firms, although relatively small in size, are confronted with a complex nationwide array of taxes. Forty-five states and the District of Columbia require out-of-state sellers to collect a use tax, and there are many differing tests of liability. In addition, thousands of local jurisdictions impose sales taxes of varying amounts, making it impossible, it is claimed, for small firms to keep up with every applicable tax law. Advocates insist that it is highly important to firms engaged in interstate sales and to freedom of commerce and the economic benefits that flow therefrom for sellers to have, so far as possible, clear-cut and uniform sales and use tax guidelines. Sellers whose activities do not exceed the minimum standards set out in S. 983 have no significant presence in the taxing jurisdiction, and, advocates claim, no state under these circumstances provides services to the seller that justify imposing a tax or collection burden on the seller. The proposed rules are also defended as clearly defining business location to eliminate the possibility that two states considering the same set of facts will tax the same transaction. Special provisions to eliminate collection burdens for out-of-state sellers whose sales are below a certain threshold and to permit out-of-state sellers of less than $100,000 in a state to rely on the buyer's certification of the local sales or use tax rate are defended as easing the burden of compliance on businesses of smaller size. Collections by many firms are so small, proponents claim, that the states cannot afford to police their activities. Greater clarity in the guidelines, it is argued, would help end the abusive practices of some states which demand tax payments and issue tax assessments and penalty notices without knowing in fact whether a sales tax is due or whether an obligation to collect the use tax exists.[93]

Views of the Opponents on Ground Rules for Sales and Use Taxes. Eugene F. Corrigan, executive director of the Multistate Tax Commission, argues that S. 983 does not really do anything for small mail order firms, since no state has the authority to impose sales taxes or require the collection of use taxes if the seller has no payroll or property in the state, if sales are effected through mailing a catalog, and if orders are filled by mail or by common carrier delivery from outside the state. But, according to Corrigan, neither will adoption of the proposed legislation stop state authorities from seeking to make out-of-state sellers register and report for sales and use tax purposes.[94] Some states are particularly concerned about provisions in S. 983 that would bar the imposition of tax collection responsibility on a firm unless the out-of-state seller has a business location in the state or regularly makes household deliveries in the state. This provision would appear to overrule the Supreme Court's *Scripto* decision.

Some state and local taxing authorities believe that solicitation of sales within the taxing jurisdiction by *any* representative of the seller should be a sufficient basis for imposing sales and use taxes. Many firms, it is claimed, do not store goods within a state, but purchases are made because of the efforts of such firms' authorized dealers and agents within the state. Denying the right to impose tax collection responsibility in these cases, it is claimed, cannot be rationally defended. David C. Hardesty, Jr., tax commissioner for West Virginia, points out that multistate corporations frequently do not treat his state as a separate sales area, chiefly because of West Virginia's special geographical configuration. S. 983 would sanction continued solicitation by out-of-state company representatives without their establishing a company place of business in West Virginia, thus denying normal sales and use tax revenues to the state.

Opponents of S. 983 also criticize the provisions of the bill that would treat consignment sales as not involving sellers' stock within the jurisdiction, thus denying the right to tax them. In addition, opponents attack the provision of the bill that would excuse the seller from collecting use taxes if the purchaser furnishes a registration number or other identification showing that it is registered with the taxing jurisdiction to collect or pay a use tax in the taxing state. This, opponents argue, would allow buyers to obtain goods tax-free and allow sellers to avoid their duty to collect a use tax without any showing that the buyer's submission was furnished in good faith and without certification that the goods were in fact intended for resale. In sum, many of the bill's provisions, according to opponents, will simply aid firms that seek to evade state taxes.[95]

Opponents of S. 983 also maintain that states are frequently whipsawed by those who claim that they have paid taxes in another state and that the bill would only make matters worse. The bill, it is claimed, would enable out-of-state sellers, particularly in highly populated border areas, to sell products tax-free, thus underpricing local merchants, who must collect sales taxes. The competitive position of intrastate businesses depends on effective enforcement of the use tax, but S. 983, it is claimed, would create so many loopholes that the ability of the states and localities to raise revenues through this tax would be seriously impaired.

The bill's prohibition against including interstate shipping charges for the purpose of determining the sales or use tax would also discriminate against in-state sellers, according to opponents. William Barnes, chief of the Sales and Income Tax Division of the Mississippi State Tax Commission, has cited the example of an in-state seller who fills an order in Mississippi by ordering steel from Pennsylvania. The freight charges are a cost to him. These charges are included in the retail sales price, and a sales tax is collected on the total. But an out-of-state seller could avoid collecting the use tax, under the terms of the bill, on as much of the sales price as involves freight charges. Mississippi law requires freight charges to be included, primarily as an equalizing factor for the sales tax levy that must be collected by the in-state merchant, and to nullify this state law would add to the bill's discrimination against in-state sellers.[96]

Opponents also claim that the provision of S. 983 that would excuse out-of-state sellers from classifying sales according to geographic area within a state, unless the destination is a political subdivision in which the seller has a business location or regularly makes household deliveries, would deprive many local jurisdictions of revenues that would otherwise be earmarked for them. Edgar L. Lindley, commissioner of the Ohio Department of Taxation, notes that forty-two of the eighty-eight counties in Ohio, for example, have sales and use taxes and that these local levies are normally collected by the state. This provision of the bill would make it impossible, in most instances, for the state to distribute the proceeds of use tax collections to the appropriate county or other subdivision. In-state sellers would be discriminated against, because they would continue to be obligated to collect taxes regardless of the volume of their sales. Other state officials criticize the bill for failing to provide uniformity of treatment, since it does not include leases and rentals of personal property or service contracts. Clark estimates that Indiana would lose $50 million a year in sales and use tax revenues overall if the bill were enacted.[97]

Proponents' Rejoinder to Opponents' Arguments on Ground Rules. Advocates of the bill agree that mail order firms that do not have places of business within a state or regularly deliver to households within the state are not subject to the provisions of that state's sales and use tax laws, but they reject their opponents' claim that the presence of *any* sales representative in the state should constitute a sufficient nexus with the state to permit taxation, noting the Supreme Court's reliance on the due process clause to invalidate the imposition of taxes when there are insignificant contacts. Proponents claim that there is a great deal of uncertainty as to when states and localities may properly impose such taxes, and that the proposed legislation would provide uniformity and certainty in the law and enable sellers to resist improper tax and penalty impositions. Consignment sales, it is argued, should not be subject to tax when a final sale of a comparable product involving the same buyer and seller would not be taxed. The buyer certification plan would ease compliance burdens on smaller businesses, but firms with larger sales volumes would have to collect taxes for states and localities without the benefit of these special provisions. The bill is necessary, it is claimed, to avoid the overwhelming burden of collecting and accounting for taxes now imposed on smaller interstate firms and the burden of duplicate taxes on some products sold interstate, burdens that place interstate sales at a disadvantage. Advocates also believe that state estimates of revenue losses are overstated and that in fact the costs to sellers of collecting taxes for small quantities of goods may outweigh the taxes collected. Thomas J. McHugh, a vice president of taxes of Kraft, Inc., maintains that sellers the size of his firm are not reluctant to collect and remit taxes if the procedure and requirements are readily understandable and administratively workable. In his view, buyer certification and other provisions of the bill have the potential to increase state and local revenues as a result of greater tax compliance by sellers.[98]

Proponents claim that excluding interstate transportation charges from the price of an article subject to state sales or use taxes is fair, since interstate transportation charges are usually much higher than intrastate transportation charges. As to the concern of states such as West Virginia that sellers will evade state taxes by locating their places of business outside the state, proponents claim that section 102 of S. 983 would permit states to enter into cooperative agreements to prevent such evasion.

Views of Proponents on Restricting the Imposition of Gross Receipts Taxes. Advocates of this provision in S. 983 contend that the *Standard Pressed Steel* decision made the determination of whether a corporation had a sufficient nexus with the taxing jurisdiction more complicated and that a firm should be able to have an office within a state without incurring liability for the gross receipts tax unless the office is directly involved in selling activities. The proposed legislation, if enacted, would return the law as to nexus to its status before *Standard Pressed Steel* and substantially adopt the Court's *Norton* decision as the touchstone for nexus.[99]

Advocates of this change contend that gross receipts taxes are a growing problem for interstate businesses and one of the principal needs is legislation to clearly delineate when a taxing jurisdiction may impose a gross receipts tax and which state has authority to tax the gross receipts from a particular sale, since in some instances two states seek to impose a gross receipts tax on the same sale. Businesses, proponents argue, need this certainty so they will know when to accrue funds for the payment of the tax and how to avoid double taxation.[100]

Views of Opponents on Restricting the Imposition of Gross Receipts Taxes. Opponents of the provisions of S. 983 that deal with gross receipts taxes maintain that the proposed limitation is unjustified, since a nonresident firm can cultivate an in-state market without establishing a business office as that term is defined in the bill. They contend that the focus of attention should be the nature and quality of the contacts of the out-of-state firm in the state. Opponents note that in the *Standard Pressed Steel* case the court cited the benefits provided by the state to the out-of-state firm. S. 983, in their view, leaves too much room for avoidance of taxes while still permitting an out-of-state firm to enjoy a large in-state market. This gives the out-of-state seller an unfair advantage over the in-state business that must pay the gross receipts tax.[101]

Compliance Costs and Administrative Burdens

Advocates' Arguments as to the Legislation's Costs and Burdens as to Income Taxes. State taxation of income through the use of nationwide or worldwide combination accounting is singled out by the advocates of federal legislation for particular criticism. They contend that state and local taxation of multistate and multinational corporations has resulted in an avalanche of unnecessary paperwork for businesses of all sizes. They also point to the unusual problems in determining whether a firm and its affiliated firms are engaged in a unitary business. This conclusion must be derived from an enormous number of facts about all aspects of the companies' operations and there is a lack of objective standards for determining this question. The difficulty is compounded when a foreign parent corporation is involved, and states tax worldwide operations on the basis of the unitary principle.[102]

Additional problems are involved in determining taxable income. Among the serious problems when foreign subsidiaries or foreign parents of U.S. corporations are involved, for example, are those of language differences, levels of inflation, and when and how foreign exchange rates are to be calculated. Differences in accounting methods, it is argued, may mean that transactions between affiliated corporations will not wash out—losses may become gains, and vice versa. Consolidated reporting of the income of accrual-basis companies with that of cash-basis companies may dramatically alter the tax picture. Also, there are differences from country to country in the treatment of depreciation, capital consumption, and capital recovery allocations. Some countries permit the immediate expensing of capital expenditures, while others have varying depreciation requirements, and this makes income comparisons difficult.[103] Proponents cite the statement of Donald Lubick, former deputy assistant secretary of the Treasury for tax policy, to the effect that if U.S. companies doing business in Japan had to translate all of their subsidiaries' income into yen and convert to Japanese accounting methods, and this included subsidiaries that had no transactions with Japan, the administrative burdens would be almost insuperable, thus making it very difficult for the United States to continue as an important nation in world commerce.[104]

Additional problems are involved for the taxpaying company in obtaining required information from foreign sources, particularly from a foreign parent corporation, since the foreign country's laws may prohibit the parent's disclosure of various items of information. Yet a company may suffer substantial state penalties for failure to comply with state demands for information. These and other problems, it is claimed, are causing companies to go to court in unprecedented numbers, and hundreds of new court decisions only add to the confusion. Some cases may pend in court for ten years or longer, thus giving no guidance to the participants regarding future years' taxes.[105] Advocates also cite the widely differing interpretations that state courts have given Public Law 86–272 and the burdens that this situation places on firms that operate in interstate commerce. Senator Mathias has argued that federal legislation dealing with income from foreign sources is needed to reduce the paperwork burden on companies. Clear and uniform rules would also save much time and cost in computing the tax base and applying the state's apportionment formula. Adoption of the pending legislation as to income from foreign sources would also allow state and local taxing jurisdictions to rely on IRS audits to determine the amount of income subject to tax, and this would reduce their costs.[106]

Advocates' Arguments as to the Legislation's Costs and Burdens as to Sales and Use Taxes. Federal legislation to standardize the rules as to when interstate businesses must collect sales and use taxes and to simplify the rules and the forms employed in collecting and reporting also has a high priority with the critics of state and local tax laws. The problems small businesses have with complex and varying tax laws and with the proliferation of regulations, tax forms, accounting, and paperwork are said to be particularly acute, since these firms do not have the expert accountants needed to facilitate compliance. Advocates note that there may be from 7,000 to 8,000 taxing jurisdictions in the United States. Special calculations must be made and separate data must be maintained for each jurisdiction that imposes a sales or use tax, and the required reporting intervals vary from jurisdiction to jurisdiction. The president of a mail order nursery company testified that it cost his firm more than $40,000 (or more than 17 percent of collections) to collect $238,628 in taxes for two states alone.[107] S. 983, according to proponents, would deal with problems like these by setting uniform criteria for judging a firm's nexus with the taxing jurisdiction and simplifying compliance for out-of-state firms.[108]

Advocates' Arguments as to the Legislation's Costs and Burdens on Gross Receipts Taxes. Jurisdictions imposing gross receipts taxes are far less numerous than those imposing income, sales, and use taxes. However, advocates of federal legislation say that uniform standards for determining the nexus required before a jurisdiction may impose the gross receipts tax are quite important.

Advocates' Arguments as to Costs and Burdens Absent Review in Federal Court. S. 983 would establish an alternative avenue for judicial review of the issues that might be raised under this bill, if it became law, and under Public Law 86–272, namely, the U.S. Court of Claims. Advocates also cite the high percentage of state court decisions that favor the tax collectors, and the lack of uniformity in state court interpretations of Public Law 86–272 and other tax statutes as reasons for adoption of the legislation. They see review in a single court that can attain expertise in such matters as essential to achieving uniformity in interpreting the law and relieving firms of the burdens of litigating in a multiplicity of jurisdictions. Review de novo by the Court of Claims is also required, it is argued, to help reduce administrative costs.[109]

Opponents' Arguments as to the Legislation's Costs and Burdens as to State Income Taxes. Opponents criticize the pending bills on grounds that their provisions concerning income taxes would compel the use of the separate accounting method with arm's-length adjustments in intercompany transactions to determine the ceiling on the tax base. First, however, firms would have to compute their income taxes by the method required in the particular state, thus, in effect, doubling the cost and burden of completing tax returns. The arm's-length method is criticized as inefficient, costly to police, and inadequate to deal with increasingly sophisticated multinational corporate structures. The arm's-length method is complex; IRS litigation with one multinational over arm's-length adjustments is claimed to have cost $10 million and taken more than ten years. The application of worldwide combination accounting relieves both the state and the corporation of the need to construct a hypothetical profit and loss statement for each state based on hypothetical intragroup charges for goods, services, and capital by affiliates outside the state.[110]

Some opponents acknowledge that worldwide combination accounting poses special disclosure burdens and heavy compliance expenses on the foreign parents of approximately 600 U.S. firms. Some measure of relief may be necessary for these foreign firms, these opponents say, but the 4,500 U.S. corporations that own foreign subsidiaries already provide the Internal Revenue Service with much of the data needed to implement worldwide combination accounting, and this information is reported regularly and in dollars. These firms, according to opponents, should not be excused from state reporting requirements.

Donald C. Lubick acknowledged that perhaps the states, like the federal government, should allow a foreign tax credit for taxes paid or deemed paid, but he noted that this would require coordination of foreign tax credits among the states and with the federal government. This would be complex and create still other problems of compliance.[111]

Opponents' Arguments as to the Legislation's Costs and Burdens as to Sales and Use Taxes. Opponents of the pending legislation say that under current procedures the states can minimize the manpower devoted to sales and use tax enforcement by imposing liability on sellers unless they can affirmatively show either proper collection or proper exemption. The state presumes liability unless the seller can show careful recordkeeping. S. 983 would shift much of the state's concentration on the relatively few sellers who would escape collection of the use tax under the new ground rules as to nexus to a concentration on the thousands of users within the state who receive products from those out-of-state sellers. Those out-of-state sellers who remained subject to liability for collection of the use tax would no longer have to indicate the local jurisdictions in which sales were made if they had no place of business in them and did not regularly make household deliveries to them. This would make enforcement and auditing of interstate sales virtually impossible, according to opponents. Greatly increased manpower would have to be devoted to establishing nexus, to auditing, and to enforcing collections generally. Opponents argue that the out-of-state seller's cost of collecting the use tax should be treated as a normal cost of doing business. Thus, it could be written off on federal and state tax returns. Firms with a small volume of sales should not be given a special break, for these out-of-state sellers receive the same benefits of police protection and so forth from the receiving state that large firms receive. These sellers would not expand their operations to include sales in these jurisdictions, it is claimed, unless it were profitable to do so.[112]

Opponents' Arguments as to Review in the Court of Claims. Opponents of S. 983 attack its provision for review in the U.S. Court of Claims, insisting that state courts are adequate to deal with these issues and that if litigants are dissatisfied with state court decisions they can seek review in the Supreme Court. Requiring de novo review would render the determinations of state taxing authorities meaningless. Such review, it is claimed, would cause a major increase in litigation expenses for all parties involved, since the normal deference afforded administrative decisions would not be granted.[113]

Advocates' Rejoinder to Opponents' Contentions on Costs and Burdens. Proponents dispute the claim that the proposed legislation would complicate income accounting or double the work of completing income tax returns. Advocates note that all multinational corporations already use the separate accounting method for internal business purposes and, more important, that it is the system used to determine federal income taxes. It is recognized by our principal trading partners and in the international community. The separate accounting system with arm's-length adjustments has some complexity, but, advocates claim, its problems are well understood, recordkeeping is not multiplied beyond reasonable limits, and this method prevents any significant double taxation.[114]

Effect on Commerce and Economic Efficiency

The effect of the proposed changes on interstate and foreign commerce, and on economic efficiency generally are also the subject of continuing debate.

Views of Proponents as to the Effects of the Proposals on Commerce and Efficiency. Advocates insist that S. 983 would encourage interstate business by removing unjustified burdens on such commerce and by permitting comparative economic advantage rather than tax policy to govern business location decisions. The proponents make these specific points:

The legislation would remove factors that discourage interstate trade and commerce. Senator Mathias calls the current system of state and local taxation of multistate corporations inefficient and outmoded. Representative James T. Broyhill (R-N.C.) contends that the system forces firms to deal with increasing amounts of paperwork and there is decreasing predictability and certainty as to corporate tax liability. Such uncertainties cannot help but undermine efficiency, in his view, and the public has to pay for the extra paperwork and inefficiency through higher prices. Senator Mathias states: "I find it ironic that taxation—a factor we have the power to control completely, a factor that could be simple, straightforward and predictable—is kept complex, fraught with uncertainty, and in a constant state of flux." He contends that S. 983 would promote greater uniformity and certainty and help smooth the flow of interstate commerce. Some interstate firms contend that the current taxing and tax-dunning practices of some jurisdictions that impose sales, use, and gross receipts taxes successfully deter them from doing business in those jurisdictions and thus restrain interstate trade. A witness for the National Association of Manufacturers contended that lack of uniformity among the states is an obstacle to the free flow of commerce, and that lack of reform and an avalanche of paper work may fractionalize the United States through burdens on and barriers to interstate trade. Adoption of the proposed legislation, it is claimed, would lessen the trend toward state protectionism and permit free market forces to promote allocative efficiency.[115]

The legislation would allow comparative economic advantage to determine locational decisions. Proponents of federal legislation maintain that the establishment of new manufacturing facilities in a state has a multiplier effect on employment, since two jobs may be created in the community outside the factory for every new job within the factory. But some states have so abused the unitary business principle and combined accounting, it is asserted, that firms that would otherwise locate new facilities in these states do not do so. More important, in the eyes of proponents, is the need for certainty and fairness in state and local tax laws so that locational and other business decisions will be based primarily on efficiency considerations. The principle of comparative advantage would then provide the optimal level of production at the least cost, with consequent reduction in prices to consumers.

Views of Opponents as to the Effects of the Proposals on Commerce and Efficiency. Opponents insist that the states must be free to set tax policy without federal restraints and that, in any event, their tax policies have little influence on businesses' locational decisions. They say this about the proposals:

Bills would deny states the freedom to set tax policy. Opponents maintain that states and localities must be free to fashion their tax programs to meet their own special needs. There will always be differences in tax treatment from state to state and from community to community in a federal system such as ours. Diversity must not be stifled, and the states should be permitted to solve problems in this area through cooperative action.

Tax policies have little influence on firms' locational decisions. Differences in tax policies from state to state are greatly overemphasized, opponents claim, in terms of their effect on the location of businesses. These decisions, it is claimed, are primarily influenced by the general business climate rather than by tax differences. A recent study by the Advisory Commission on Intergovernmental Relations (ACIR) is cited to show that businesses are more concerned about land and building costs, transportation facilities, wage rates, right-to-work laws, the relative importance of labor unions, proximity to markets and to raw materials, and the availability of community services than they are about state and local taxes. The taxes that do concern business firms, according to this study, are income taxes and property taxes, but the latter are not dealt with in the reform proposals. The ACIR report notes that over a six-year period only 554 manufacturing firms out of a total of 140,000 moved from one state to another. Thus, while state and local taxes can be a swing factor when other advantages and disadvantages weigh equally, opponents contend such taxes count for much less than such things as wage rates.[116]

Proponents' Rejoinder. Proponents respond to the claim that taxes have little influence on business location decisions by noting that opponents rely on the relatively few instances in which established industrial firms have relocated in other regions or states. More significant, in their view, is the fact that foreign corporations seeking plant sites in this country avoid states that spread their income tax net too widely.[117] They also note that, notwithstanding the claim that taxes have little influence on business location decisions, many states have set up programs of tax abatement to lure industry. Proponents maintain, moreover, that the burdens of collecting and reporting sales and use taxes and gross receipts taxes, and the barriers to interstate commerce created by these taxes, cannot be explained away by state and local authorities. Economic efficiency, it is claimed, clearly would be advanced in the context of interstate commerce by the adoption of S. 983.

Views of Proponents as to the Effects of the Proposals on State and Local Taxation of Income from Foreign Sources. Advocates of the bills contend that enactment is necessary to promote economic efficiency and international trade.

More specifically, proponents make the following arguments:

The legislation would allow the United States to compete more effectively in the international marketplace. If Congress wants to encourage international trade, proponents claim, it must protect U.S. corporations and their affiliates from double taxation. An efficient and predictable tax system is a must if we are to compete successfully internationally. The United States, according to Senator Mathias, is no longer dominant in the world marketplace and cannot afford to cripple American businesses through an irrational tax system.[118] It is important that we halt the trend toward state protectionism and develop a coherent international trade policy. Tax policy should not work at cross-purposes with that of trade policy. Tax policy affecting international trade should, in this view, be consistent at all levels of government.[119]

Advocates also maintain that U.S. firms cannot compete in the world market if they face higher effective tax rates than their foreign competitors. They contend that it is a tenet of international tax law and practice that income from foreign sources is taxed by the home country only when it is repatriated and point out that some countries do not tax such income at all. Taxation on repatriation is the practice of the federal government, but several states tax income regardless of whether it is or can be repatriated, and most states fail to allow a tax credit for taxes that have already been paid to foreign governments on the same income. In addition, some states tax corporations based on worldwide combined reporting, thus apportioning to themselves the incomes of affiliated corporations that may have no contacts with the taxing jurisdictions other than their relationship to a corporation that does do business or is domiciled there, thus taking income that is also taxed abroad.[120] Advocates insist that, if our businesses are to penetrate foreign markets and compete effectively for those markets, our tax practices, state and federal, must not place us at a competitive disadvantage as they now do for it is the economies of competing nations that encourage their companies to invest abroad that will benefit. Tax policies that weaken our international competitive position will, in the long run, adversely affect U.S. employment, the balance of payments, and the domestic economy in general.

Proponents cite the view of Norman Ture, now undersecretary of the Treasury for economic and tax policy, that the appropriate tax on corporations would be one that imposed tax liabilities on business firms in proportion to the costs imposed on the economy of the taxing country. This principle and the principle of tax neutrality, according to Ture, mean that there should be no federal tax on income from foreign sources.[121] Advocates argue that this reasoning is equally applicable to state taxes on income from foreign sources and Congress should ban application of worldwide combination accounting and taxing income from foreign sources.

Advocates of federal legislation insist that if tax policy is neutral, international firms will locate their operations where pretax returns on investment are the greatest. Thus, if American firms establish operations abroad they do so to take advantage of access to natural resources, lower labor and other costs, or some other advantage. These differences in profitability and in costs of production are the fundamental basis of world trade. Advocates argue that the economic principle of comparative advantage should be permitted to work in the world economy, since this permits each country to specialize in the things it does best, thereby increasing overall efficiency. This international division of labor, according to proponents, would maximize world output at the least overall cost and to the greatest benefit of mankind. The principle of comparative advantage is vital to American businesses in the long run.[122] Thus, tax policy should allow a free flow of capital and commerce and permit American firms and their affiliates to compete aggressively for international markets.

Continued use of the unitary tax principle with worldwide combination accounting, according to advocates, is a destabilizing factor in international relations and foreign trade. Countries such as the United Kingdom, Canada, Japan, and Switzerland have voiced concern over the application of worldwide combination accounting. Proponents fear that failure to enact corrective legislation may provoke other nations to adopt worldwide combination accounting, action that would have a disastrous effect on the international flow of trade and capital.[123]

The legislation would have a beneficial effect on the domestic economy. Proponents contend that tax policies that weaken our competitive position in world trade will reduce domestic employment and weaken the domestic economy. The excessive expense of complying with state and local tax laws and the imposition, in effect, of a penalty tax rate higher than normal through the unitary tax principle and worldwide combination accounting hurts American companies. These factors, it is claimed, discourage investment in states employing the unitary principle even when these states may be the appropriate site for new plants under the principle of comparative advantage. J. Robert Vastine of the California Council for International Trade maintains that overzealous use of worldwide combination accounting by his state has impaired its ability to attract new businesses. Restricting worldwide combination accounting, in his view, would bring more than enough new investment to California to offset any tax revenue loss from the change.[124] Enactment of federal legislation, according to Senator Mathias, would provide new incentives for investment in other jurisdictions as well and new job opportunities that would produce tax revenues far outweighing the possible revenue loss.[125]

Views of Opponents on the Effects of the Proposals on State and Local Taxation of Income from Foreign Sources. Opponents maintain that provisions of the federal tax law that permit deferral of taxes on income from foreign sources until it is repatriated and that allow a foreign tax credit stimulate foreign investment at the expense of investment in this country. The deferral of taxation until income is repatriated, according to opponents, gives the businesses involved the benefit of what is, in effect, a tax-free loan, since these earnings can draw interest while retained overseas, a benefit not available to corporations that operate only in the United States. Deferral, one scholar estimates, reduces the effective rate of federal tax on income from foreign sources some 10 percent below the statutory rate of 46 percent.[126] Opponents note that the Kennedy and Carter administrations proposed elimination of tax deferral on income from foreign sources, and that amendments were adopted in 1962 that limited the accumulation of unrepatriated dividends and eliminated federal deferral for certain categories of income earned by "controlled foreign corporations."[127]

The foreign tax credit provided by the federal government, it is claimed, also favors foreign investment over domestic investment because a firm doing business solely in the United States can deduct only state and local taxes from its earned income while the multinational firm obtains a more valuable dollar-for-dollar credit for taxes paid to foreign governments. Through the foreign tax credit, it is argued, the federal government relinquishes its right to tax revenues when foreign taxes exceed the federal corporate tax rate and gives up tax revenues proportionately when foreign taxes are lower. H.R. 1983 and S. 655 would force the states to do the same.[128]

Opponents contend that deferral and the foreign tax credit should not be extended to state and local taxation of foreign source dividends. Opponents cite the explanation of Senator Vance Hartke (D-Ind.) of the provisions of the Burke-Hartke bill that would have eliminated deferral and repealed the foreign tax credit provided in federal law:

> At present, our tax laws make an overseas investment more attractive than one in Indiana or New York. For example, profits

earned by a foreign subsidiary of an American firm are not taxed until they are repatriated. To the extent that the firm does pay taxes to a foreign government, these taxes count as a dollar-for-dollar credit against any federal tax liability.

Profits made in Indiana are taxed when earned. And taxes paid to the State of Indiana can only be taken as deductions against gross income rather than as a federal tax credit. My bill will plug both of these gaping loopholes through which American capital, technology, and jobs have poured [overseas].[129]

They also cite the statement of Donald Lubick that bills "limiting state taxation to U.S. source income may tilt the tax incentives toward foreign investment and employment."[130] H.R. 1983 and S. 655, according to opponents, would also weaken the U.S. balance of payments position by encouraging companies to keep their foreign earnings abroad. Opponents claim that multinational firms would restructure their corporate organization so that as much income as possible would come from the earnings of foreign subsidiaries, thus favoring foreign investment over domestic investment even more.[131]

During the 96th Congress, Senator Frank Church (D-Idaho) referred to bills to regulate state taxation of interstate and international commerce as granting new tax incentives that would encourage the movement of jobs abroad. Opponents also note that in the case of two projects that provide the same after-tax return to investors, one overseas and one in this country, the project in this country would be more beneficial because it would provide greater tax revenues.[132] They cite data showing that as much as 44 percent of U.S. foreign investment may be in manufacturing and argue that such investment necessarily worsens the terms of trade for similar products exported by U.S. manufacturers.[133] When foreign investment produces products that are imported into this country in direct competition with similar products produced here, a special hurt is inflicted on the domestic firms producing those products. Therefore, according to opponents, these funds should be invested in this country to provide jobs and greater tax revenues. Federal regulation of state and local taxation of income, they say, would make direct foreign investment even more attractive than it is now.

Proponents' Rejoinder. Proponents of the pending legislation reject the argument that federal tax law discriminates against domestic investment by U.S. companies in favor of foreign investment. First, they say, opponents have ignored other provisions of federal tax and trade laws that discourage foreign investment and encourage domestic investment. Accelerated depreciation, for example, can be applied to domestic assets but is not available to reduce taxes on income from foreign sources. They also point out that the investment tax credit, generally worth 10 percent of the value of new productive assets, is not available for investments abroad. Furthermore, capital gains arising from foreign operations are not treated as favorably as they are when obtained through domestic activities. The rules for carrying taxable income forward and shifting income losses backward to reduce federal taxes are less liberal in the case of foreign investments, and the percentage depletion available to domestic operations is not available to foreign subsidiaries. Finally, they note that the foreign tax credit only provides a dollar-for-dollar offset against federal taxes in cases where the foreign tax rate is equal to or less than the federal tax rate. U.S. companies investing in foreign countries with higher tax rates obtain no offset for the amount by which foreign tax rates exceed the U.S. rate. Some economic analysts estimate that income from foreign sources is taxed, on the average, at rates 20 to 30 percent above those applied to income from U.S. sources.[134]

The foreign tax credit replaced the federal tax deduction for foreign taxes in 1918. At that time, some members of Congress advocated complete elimination of federal taxes on income from foreign sources, and the credit was adopted as a compromise. Those who favor the elimination of federal taxes on income from foreign sources maintain that their position is consistent with the view that taxes should not alter the relative prices of goods traded in the private sector.[135] Deferral of taxes on foreign income until that income is repatriated, according to proponents, simply places the taxation of foreign subsidiaries of U.S. corporations on the same footing as their overseas competitors. Present U.S. revenues on income from foreign sources, judged on the basis of a tax neutrality that would allocate capital among the nations to maximize worldwide income and production, are said to be much too high.

Other factors that encourage domestic investment and discourage foreign investment include commodity taxes, tariff structures, regulatory policy, the added risk involved in foreign investments, and, of course, state and local tax policy that apportions income of affiliated firms overseas.[136] Corporate executives are primarily influenced by the risk-return potential on an investment opportunity, according to some proponents. Hence, foreign investments may be made even though the tax situation is less than favorable in order to allow a company to benefit in the event the tax laws are changed.

As to opponents' claims that current tax policy encourages the export of capital and jobs overseas and adversely affects the U.S. balance of payments, proponents respond that, given the disincentives to foreign investment cited above, the pending legislation simply seeks to redress an imbalance that discourages foreign investment and prevents us from capturing an adequate share of foreign markets. In fact, the proponents say that increasing foreign investment would not necessarily mean a reduction in domestic investment. Dan Throop Smith and Ture both point out that to assume that increased foreign investment reduces domestic investment by a like amount also means assuming that the total available for investment is inelastic, which they contend is not true. Smith notes that most corporations could borrow more money for investment than they have thus far, and therefore the commitment of funds abroad would not reduce the amount available for domestic investment. He also notes that much foreign investment by U.S. corporations and their foreign subsidiaries is accomplished with funds borrowed in foreign markets, including the Eurodollar market, and thus involves no drain on U.S. investment funds. Some corporate investment abroad involves the export of used machinery and equipment, and only scrap value can be assigned to such investment. Furthermore, some companies repatriate more income than the amount of their new investments overseas. Data for 1979 have been cited to show that American earnings on investment abroad totaled $19.4 billion that year, compared with American funds invested in foreign affiliate companies of only $5.9 billion.[137]

Nor does it follow, according to the legislation's proponents, that increased foreign investment hurts domestic employment. Foreign investment is necessary to penetrate foreign markets and to gain access to scarce minerals and other raw materials for American firms. If American companies did not invest abroad to capture foreign markets, firms from other countries would fill the void, as we have no monopoly on capital, skilled labor, marketing skills, and the like, and in time the U.S. economic position would be seriously eroded. Often, a salesman for a foreign subsidiary of a U.S. firm can sell both the products of the subsidiary and of the U.S. parent corporation, thus improving our export position and providing domestic jobs. Ture maintains that, historically, foreign investment has expanded U.S. exports because there is a tendency for foreign subsidiaries to rely on suppliers in the home jurisdiction—information on products is more readily available from such sources, and so forth.[138]

While some American jobs may be lost in some industries through the workings of the principle of comparative advantage, Milton Friedman and Dan Throop Smith contend that other jobs are created by imports into this country. These are jobs in U.S. industries producing exports that are purchased abroad with dollars earned by foreigners from the goods we import.[139]

So far as the U.S. balance of payments is concerned, advocates say that enactment of the pending legislation would help rather than hurt our position. They claim that to the extent that tax law changes stimulate investments abroad they will increase our exports, for the reasons noted above. The legislation, they argue, would also remove the disincentive to investment by foreign firms in states that now utilize the unitary business principle and worldwide combination accounting. This, according to proponents, would increase foreign investment in this country, which will provide jobs and help improve our balance-of-payments posture.[140]

Proponents contend that direct overseas investment should not be penalized because some foreign subsidiaries import products into the United States that compete with goods manufactured by American workers. Apart from the importance of the principle of comparative advantage, they note that, in any event, foreign subsidiaries sell 72 percent of their products locally in foreign countries, 22 percent in other foreign countries, and only 7 percent in the United States. The last percentage would be even smaller without shipments from Canadian affiliates under the 1965 automotive trade agreement.[141] In sum, proponents maintain that the proposals will promote both exports and economic efficiency.

Cooperative State Action versus Federal Legislation

Arguments of Those Favoring Cooperative State Action. Advocates of cooperative state action insist that our system of federalism requires the states to be free to set their own tax policies and that advocates of federal legislation ignore the substantial progress already made by the states in achieving tax uniformity. Advocates of cooperative state action view the Multistate Tax Compact as the best approach to achieving a desirable degree of uniformity. More specifically, those favoring cooperative state action argue as follows:

The legislation would curtail the freedom of states and their subdivisions to set tax policy. Advocates of cooperative state action declare that each state and community is concerned with economic development and that each must determine for itself the types of taxes, the tax base, and the level of taxes required to fund governmental activities. States and their subdivisions should be free, they insist, to tax in any way they see fit that does not offend a majority of the Supreme Court. Freedom to tax has been recognized since colonial days and is a part of our system of federalism. James B. Zagel, director of the Illinois Department of Revenue, has said that federal legislation should only be considered if its advocates can demonstrate duplicative or multiple taxation without effective judicial remedy.[142] Since the Supreme Court has made it clear that it can redress instances of duplicative taxation, no legislation is necessary.

Furthermore, state taxes have always been imposed in addition to federal taxes, and a state has never been required to grant a foreign tax credit. Federal legislation, in this view, would seriously impair the principles of federalism. It is one thing for Congress to create a preference for multijurisdictional businesses, according to proponents of cooperative state action, but it is quite another to force the states to pay for the benefits bestowed on those corporations.[143]

Opponents of federal legislation ask, in light of the foregoing, What is the legitimate federal interest in restricting state and local taxing authority? Some opponents say that, at most, the federal interest involves international relations, and any legislative action should be limited to dealing with taxes that affect the foreign parents of U.S. firms, since this is the area of international irritation.

State action has achieved substantial tax uniformity. Opponents of federal legislation say that its proponents ignore the amount of uniformity achieved in state tax practices through the Multistate Tax Compact and the Uniform Division of Income for Tax Purposes Act (UDITPA). Such uniformity is not an infringement on state sovereignty, as federal legislation would be, for it is self-imposed. A number of voluntary steps have been taken to achieve greater uniformity in state taxation, according to the National Association of Tax Administrators. Thirty-four of the forty-five states that impose corporate income taxes employ the Internal Revenue Code as the starting point for determining taxable income, and most of the remaining states have tax law provisions that in practical effect are quite like the code. Twenty-eight states follow a UDITPA approach, and most of the remaining states employ apportionment formulas that only depart from UDIPTA in some respects; all but one of the forty-one states imposing sales and use taxes allow a credit for taxes paid to another state, and twenty-six states collect local sales taxes for local governments and permit out-of-state businesses to file one tax return covering both state and local taxes.[144]

The Multistate Tax Commission is the best approach to uniformity. Opponents of federal legislation claim that the Multistate Tax Commission can achieve such further uniformity as may be desirable. They laud its joint audit program, under which a single auditor reviews a corporation's records and activities for various member states and offers uniform interpretations to aid the states. The commission promulgates regulations to aid member states, and it offers a forum to help resolve problems arising from the application of inconsistent tax rules of member states. The commission has suggested guidelines for the exchange of information on sales, use, and income taxes among the states. Nonetheless, the commission preserves state sovereignty. When a state participates in a joint audit, for example, it alone decides what action it should take as a result of the audit.[145] In sum, supporters of the commission regard it and UDITPA as the best means of achieving such further uniformity as may be desirable.[146]

Arguments of Those Favoring Federal Legislation. Advocates of federal legislation contend that state efforts to achieve uniformity have failed, that Congress has the power to regulate state and local taxation under the commerce clause, that only the federal government can conduct international relations, and that the nation should speak with one voice in foreign trade matters. They make these arguments:

State efforts to achieve tax uniformity have failed. The Uniform Division of Income for Tax Purposes Act has not brought uniformity in crucial areas, according to advocates of federal legislation, because its provisions have been interpreted differently by the states, and interstate taxation of business income therefore remains chaotic and uncoordinated. States reject or accept joint audit results depending on which action will maximize their revenues. Moreover, the Multistate Tax Compact has not achieved uniformity because, notwithstanding membership in the compact, each state is free to enact its own tax laws and free to adopt or ignore commission regulations and audit results. Advocates of federal legislation contend that the commission has failed to achieve uniformity because the compact's motivating force is the achievement of maximum state revenues without regard to the effect on interstate or international commerce or foreign relations.[147] The states have had fourteen years since the initial adoption of the compact by seven states and twenty-four years since the initial promulgation of UDITPA, yet member states of the Multistate Tax Commission remain free to do as they please and assert jurisdiction to tax as they see fit. Moreover, relatively few states have adopted the compact, and some have abandoned it. The remaining members are primarily less populous states in the West.[148]

Congress has power to regulate taxes as proposed. Senator Mathias notes that the Articles of Confederation were replaced by the Constitution, and adoption of the Constitution signified, among other things, a willingness on the part of the states to trade short-term gains for long-term progress in an orderly system of free-flowing commerce.[149] Court decisions clearly recognize the power of the Congress under the Constitution to regulate interstate and foreign commerce and to restrict or regulate state and local taxes. Congress in fact exercised that power by adopting Public Law 86–272, which serves as a precedent for the adoption of additional legislation.

The federal government is responsible for international relations, and the nation should speak with one voice on foreign trade issues. Advocates of federal legislation point out that the states cannot sign treaties or conduct international relations with foreign governments so there can be no negotiated protection of foreign corporations from arbitrary state action. The federal government has sole responsibility for international relations, and the United States, proponents claim, should speak with one voice beyond the water's edge. This will not be true if each state is free to apportion income from foreign sources. Enactment of federal legislation will ensure, according to proponents, that sensitive matters of foreign relations and trade are dealt with by the national government. Federal legislation will protect our international trade relations from the threats posed by irresponsible action on the part of some states. The states, according to proponents, cannot be permitted to formulate their own international tax policies in disregard of the national interest. If they persist in doing so, other governments may retaliate, with serious consequences for world trade generally.[150]

Lubick acknowledged that application of the unitary business principle with worldwide combination accounting has been such an irritant to international and commercial relations that we should ban its application when affiliated groups controlled by foreign persons are involved.[151] Advocates of federal legislation contend that the states and their subdivisions provide no significant benefits to the investment activities of corporations that justify their taxing foreign corporations and their activities in foreign countries through worldwide combination accounting. They also note that in *Japan Line, Ltd.* v. *County of Los Angeles,* the Supreme Court gave special weight to the risk of double taxation when foreign commerce is involved, and there is no single tribunal in which to reconcile competing claims. Advocates also note that the legislation would leave the states free to set tax rates at will, impose other taxes, and to define taxable activities so long as they do not go beyond the bounds set in the proposals. Thus, they contend that state sovereignty would be adequately preserved, as it was with the earlier enactment of Public Law 86–272.

Rejoinder of Advocates of Cooperative State Action. Those favoring cooperative state action maintain that the Supreme Court has sustained the taxing powers exercised by the states and that the states' opposition to the pending bills echoes the opposition to Public Law 86–272 as an invasion of the states' inherent right to levy needed taxes, an opposition that was expressed by a minority of the Senate Finance Committee in 1959.[152]

NOTES TO TEXT

[1] See, for example, Northwestern States Portland Cement Company v. Minnesota, 358 U.S. 450, 457, 476–77 (1958); Moorman Manufacturing Co. v. Bair, 437 U.S. 267, 280 (1978).

[2] See, for example, Spector Motor Service v. O'Connor, 340 U.S. 602 (1951); Railway Express Agency v. Virginia, 347 U.S. 359 (1954). Virginia reworded its statute to avoid the "Spector rule," and that statute was sustained in Railway Express Agency v. Virginia, 358 U.S. 434 (1959). The decision in the *Spector* case was overruled in Complete Auto Transit, Inc. v. Brady, 430 U.S. 274 (1976). The Court will now sustain a state tax statute if there is a sufficient nexus with the state and the tax does not discriminate against interstate commerce, is fairly apportioned, and is not unrelated to the services the state provides the taxpayer.

[3] 216 U.S. 1 (1909).

[4] Looney v. Crane Co., 245 U.S. 178 (1917); International Paper Co. v. Massachusetts, 246 U.S. 135, 142 (1917).

[5] 390 U.S. 317, 324, 326 (1962). The Court noted that, as far as due process is concerned, the only question is whether the tax in practical operation is related to the opportunities, benefits, or protections conferred or afforded by the taxing state, and this requirement is satisfied if the tax is fairly apportioned to the commerce carried on within the state. In this particular case, however, the mileage method of apportionment resulted in gross overreaching and thus cast a burden on property located outside the borders of the state. Ibid., pp. 324–26, and note 5 at page 324. In Colonial Pipeline Co. v. Traigle, 421 U.S. 100 (1975), the Court noted that the mere act of carrying on business in interstate commerce does not exempt a corporation from state taxation, and it sustained a nondiscriminatory state corporate franchise tax on a showing that a corporation that engaged only in interstate commerce gained benefits and protections of value and importance to its business from the state. In the *Moorman* case, cited in note 1, the Court refused to strike down an income allocation formula that, because of differing state formulas, produced some risk of duplication of taxes, absent a showing of actual duplication or arbitrary results.

[6] *Significant Features of Fiscal Federalism 1979–80* (Washington, D.C.: Advisory Commission on Intergovernmental Relations, 1980), pp. 72, 134–39.

[7] Justice John Paul Stevens states this proposition as follows: "It is fundamental that a state has no power to impose a tax on income earned outside of the state." Mobil Oil Corp. v. Commissioner of Taxes of Vermont, 445 U.S. 425, 451 (1980), dissent of Justice Stevens and note 4 to his dissenting opinion.

[8] Frank M. Keesling and John S. Warren, "The Unitary Concept in the Allocation of Income," *Hastings Law Journal,* vol. 12 (August 1960), p. 42.

[9] Recalculation of the value of goods and services transferred from one firm to another is accomplished to reflect arm's-length values under the authority of 26 U.S.C. 482.

[10] Keesling and Warren, "The Unitary Concept," p. 46.

[11] States that apply the unitary concept to domestic corporations include Alaska*, Arizona, Arkansas, California*, Colorado*, Florida*, Idaho*, Illinois, Indiana, Iowa, Kansas*, Kentucky, Maine, Massachusetts, Mississippi*, Montana*, Nebraska*, New Hampshire*, New York*, North Carolina, North Dakota*, Oklahoma*, Oregon*, Utah*, Virginia, and West Virginia. The states marked with an asterisk apply the concept frequently. States which apply the unitary concept to corporations worldwide include Alaska, California, Colorado, Idaho, Montana, North Dakota, Oregon, and Utah.

[12] Six states use an apportionment formula other than an equally weighted three-factor formula—property, payroll, sales. The states that use a double-weighted sales factor are Florida, Massachusetts, New York, and Wisconsin. West Virginia uses a two-factor formula (property and payroll), while Iowa uses a one-factor formula (sales).

[13] 358 U.S. 450 (1959).

[14] 437 U.S. 267 (1978).

[15] 447 U.S. 207 (1980).

[16] In the *Moorman* case the Court said: "Appellant does not suggest that it has shown that a significant portion of the income attributed to Iowa in fact was generated by its Illinois operations; the record does not contain any separate accounting analysis showing what portion of appellant's profits was attributable to sales, to manufacturing, or to any other phase of the company's operations." 437 U.S. 267, 272. In the *Exxon* case (note 15) the company relied on this language as sanctioning its use of the separate accounting approach to demonstrate that the Wisconsin practice improperly apportions out-of-state income to Wisconsin. The *Exxon* decision thus closed the door left ajar by the language quoted from the *Moorman* decision.

[17] U.S., Congress, House of Representatives, Committee on Ways and Means, *Hearings on State Taxation of Foreign Source Income,* 96th Congress, 2d session, March 31, 1980 (hereafter cited as *1980 House Hearings on State Taxation of Foreign Source Income*), p. 156, statement of Ernest S. Christian, Jr., Committee on State Taxation, Council of State Chambers of Commerce. For purposes of this analysis the word "dividend" means a distribution made by a firm out of its earnings or profits, or from any other source that does not impair capital, to its stockholders in proportion to their shares of stock or to their membership interest in the firm. Compare 26 U.S.C. 316.

[18] Senator Charles McC. Mathias, Jr. (R-Md.), "Reporting State Tax Liability," *Congressional Record,* vol. 127 (January 19, 1981), pp. S 300–301, quoting a statement of the tax section of the New York Bar Association. For a detailed survey of state law, see *A Study of the Income Tax Treatment Afforded Dividend Income by the Individual States* (Washington, D.C.: Committee on State Taxation of the Council of State Chambers of Commerce, 1980).

[19] If the states were to follow the federal pattern of intercorporate dividend taxation, a state would provide an 85 percent or 100 percent deduction for dividends received from corporations subject to tax in the state. It would provide a tax credit to corporations domiciled within the state for dividends received from nondomiciled subsidiaries to offset income taxes paid to other jurisdictions by the nondomiciled subsidiaries. Dividends received by nondomiciled corporations doing business in the state from other nondomiciled corporations, because of credit allowed for taxes previously paid, would only be taxed in rare circumstances. The statement of the tax section of the New York Bar Association cited in the previous footnote reasons that there is widespread duplicative taxation by the states because most states have adopted the federal tax law definition of taxable income as a starting point

for fixing state taxable income and in doing so they have also paralleled the federal rule by including foreign source dividends in the income base. They do not follow the second part of the federal rule, which is to allow some type of credit for foreign taxes paid and which is the reason why the foreign source dividends are included in the federal income base in the first place. The statement notes, in addition, that the tax rates of many foreign countries that are major trading partners of the United States are higher than state tax rates, and argues that the states are unwilling to grant a credit that might wipe out state tax liability.

[20] 445 U.S. 425 (1980).

[21] Ibid., pp. 458–61.

[22] A seller who fails to collect the use tax may be personally liable for its payment. Use tax statutes frequently have provisions to prevent duplication of the tax, and they may provide offsets for amounts that have been paid to another state. See Scripto v. Carson, 362 U.S. 207, 210 (1960).

[23] Advisory Commission on Intergovernmental Relations, *Significant Features of Fiscal Federalism,* pp. 72, 79, 108.

[24] 362 U.S. 207 (1960).

[25] 386 U.S. 753 (1967).

[26] Ibid., pp. 759–60.

[27] 430 U.S. 551 (1977).

[28] U.S., Congress, Senate, Committee on the Judiciary, *Hearings on Interstate Taxation,* 95th Congress, 1st and 2d sessions, December 5, 1977 through December 20, 1978 (hereafter cited as *Senate Hearings on Interstate Taxation*), pp. 126–31, statement of Louis R. Marchese, representing the Automobile Service Industry Association and the National Association of Wholesaler-Distributors. This witness detailed the varying provisions of state law for sixteen states.

[29] 340 U.S. 534, 537 (1951).

[30] 419 U.S. 560 (1975).

[31] Of related interest is the Supreme Court's treatment of the states' power to collect a tax on the value of property shipped into a state by an out-of-state seller. In Michelin Tire Corp. v. Wages, 423 U.S. 276 (1976), the Court overruled its earlier decision under the import-export clause of the U.S. Constitution, article 1, section 10, clause 2, which held that a foreign importer's products were immune from taxation in the receiving state while stored in their original form or in the original package. In sustaining the nondiscriminatory ad valorem tax involved, the Court relied on the circumstance that the foreign importer's storage of its products in a warehouse in the receiving state for distribution on a wholesale basis was no different from storage by a domestic wholesaler whose products were subject to the ad valorem tax. In Japan Line, Ltd. v. County of Los Angeles, 441 U.S. 434 (1979), the Court was confronted with the question of whether political subdivisions of a state could collect nondiscriminatory taxes on the value of shipping containers owned by foreign shipping lines and taxable in full in the home port country of those shipping lines. The solicitor general elected to file a friend-of-court brief with the Supreme Court because of the foreign relations and foreign trade implications of the case. The taxing jurisdictions relied heavily upon the Court's prior abandonment of the "home port doctrine" that gave the home state of equipment moving in interstate commerce exclusive authority to levy an ad valorem tax on such equipment except for ocean-going vessels, and approval of the apportionment of

taxes on such equipment among the states, citing in particular the Court's *Moorman* decision. They also argued that there was a substantial nexus with the taxing jurisdiction, that the tax did not discriminate against interstate commerce since it fell evenhandedly on all personal property in the state, and that the tax was fairly related to the services provided by the state, all points emphasized in Supreme Court cases upholding apportionment of taxes in an interstate commerce context. In this case, however, the Court concluded that double taxation of the instruments of foreign commerce was real and not just a risk, and that there was no suitable tribunal to eliminate double taxation as the Supreme Court has been able to do in cases involving equipment used solely in interstate commerce. Even a slight overlapping of taxes, as distinguished from the allowance of mathematical imprecision in apportionment among the states when only interstate commerce is involved, according to the Court, assumes great importance when sensitive matters of foreign relations and national sovereignty are involved and there is acute risk of retaliation. Thus, in this context, the Court concluded that apportionment was not permissible and that the state could not be permitted by its unilateral act to impede the nation's pursuit of its foreign relations and foreign trade objectives.

[32] 15 U.S.C. 381; Paul J. Hartman, " 'Solicitation' and 'Delivery' under Public Law 86–272," *Vanderbilt Law Review,* vol. 29 (March 1976), pp. 353, 360–61. Hartman discusses the inconsistent interpretations given this federal statute by state courts. See also notes 33 and 34.

[33] See, for example, Heublein, Inc. v. South Carolina Tax Commission, 409 U.S. 275 (1972) (local activities required by Alcoholic Beverage Control Act); Hervey v. AMF Beaird, Inc., 205 Ark. 147, 464 S.W. 2d 557 (1971) (salesmen check customer's inventories in reference to status of goods consigned for sale, collect some accounts as well as solicit sales); Clairol, Inc. v. Kingsley, 57 N.J. 199, 270 A.2d 702 (1970) (detail men and salon representatives); Olympia Brewing Co. v. Department of Revenue, 266 Ore. 309, 511 P.2d 837 (1973), cert. den., 415 U.S. 976 (beer kegs); Herff Jones Co. v. State Tax Commission, 247 Ore. 404, 430 P.2d 998 (1967) (resident salesmen collect accounts).

[34] See, for example, State ex rel. CIBA Pharmaceutical Prod., Inc. v. State Tax Commission, 382 S.W. 2d 645 (Mo. 1964); U.S. Tobacco Co. v. Commonwealth of Pennsylvania, 478 Pa. 125, 386 A.2d 471 (1978), cert. den., 439 U.S. 880.

[35] House Report 1480, 88th Congress, 2d session.

[36] The Willis bills were H.R. 11798, 89th Congress, 1st session, H.R. 16491, 89th Congress, 2d session, and H.R. 2158, 90th Congress, 1st session. Other similarly titled bills were introduced in the 90th Congress as bills "to regulate and foster commerce among the states by providing a system for the taxation of interstate commerce"as follows: S. 968 by Senator Abraham A. Ribicoff (D-Conn.); H.R. 2159 by Representative Emanuel Celler (D-N.Y.); H.R. 2160 by Representative Basil L. Whitener (D-N.C.); H.R. 2161 by Representative Robert W. Kastenmeier (D-Wis.); H.R. 2162 by Representative Jacob H. Gilbert (D-N.Y.); H.R. 2163 by Representative James C. Corman (D-Calif.); H.R. 2164 by Representative Robert B. Mathias (R-Calif.); H.R. 2165 by Representative John G. Dow (D-N.Y.); and H.R. 2166 by Representative Fred B. Rooney (D-Pa.).

[37] The Rodino bill was H.R. 7906, 91st Congress, 1st session. Additional similarly titled bills that were introduced in the 91st Congress included S. 611 by Senator Charles McC. Mathias, Jr. (R-Md.); S. 916 by Senator Ribicoff; H.R. 2179 by Representative Celler; H.R. 3835 by Representative Peter W. Rodino (D-N.J.); H.R. 4178 by Representative William M. McCulloch, Jr. (R-Ohio), and thirteen cosponsors; and H.R. 5501 by Representative Corman. Bills to "regulate commerce among the states by providing a uniform system for the application of sales and use taxes to interstate commerce" were introduced in the 91st

Congress as S. 3368 by Senators George Murphy (R-Calif.) and Alan Cranston (D-Calif.); H.R. 19580 by Representatives Burt L. Talcott (R-Calif.) and B.F. Sisk (D-Calif.); H.R. 6257 by Representative Edward J. Patten (D-N.J.); H.R. 9777 by Representative Fred B. Rooney; and H.R. 10166 by Representative Hamilton Fish, Jr. (R-N.Y.).

[38] C. R. Cahoon and William B. Brown, "The Interstate Tax Dilemma—Proposed Solution," *National Tax Journal,* vol. 26 (June 1973), pp. 187, 190. Cahoon and Brown explain briefly the terms of the principal bills introduced through 1973. See also the summary of federal legislative activity in *1980 House Hearings on State Taxation of Foreign Source Income,* pp. 294–95. The Magnuson bill was S.3333, 92d Congress, 2d session. Bills titled in the same manner as H.R. 7906 in the 91st Congress that were introduced in the 92d Congress included the following: S. 317 by Senators Ribicoff and Mathias; S. 4080 by Senator Mathias; and H.R. 1538 by Representative Rodino. Bills titled the same as S. 3368 in the 91st Congress that were introduced in the 92d Congress included S. 1210 by Senators Cranston and John V. Tunney (D-Calif.), and H.R. 4267 by Representatives Talcott and Sisk. Senators Warren G. Magnuson (D-Wash.) and Gordon Allott (R-Colo.) introduced S. 1883, a bill to permit any interstate tax compact regarding taxation of multistate taxpayers to provide a formula for taxing such taxpayers by states not entering into the compact and to require certain sellers to collect sales and use taxes.

[39] In the 93rd Congress (1973–1974) bills titled as H.R. 7906 was in the 91st Congress were introduced as follows: S. 1245 by Senators Mathias and Ribicoff, S. 1962 by Senator Magnuson, and H.R. 977 by Representative Rodino. Bills titled as S. 3368 was in the 91st Congress were introduced as follows: S. 282 by Senators Cranston and Tunney, and H.R. 1453 by Representatives Talcott and Sisk. Senator Magnuson introduced S. 2811, bearing the same title as S. 1883 in the previous Congress. Senator Walter F. Mondale (D-Minn.) introduced S. 2811 to provide a simplified uniform plan for the imposition, collection, and administration of state and local sales and use taxes with respect to interstate commerce, to reduce significantly the burden of tax compliance for persons engaged in making sales in interstate commerce, and to eliminate restrictions on the taxing powers of the states that now prevent them from securing, collecting, and remitting such taxes from certain interstate sales.

[40] See H.R. 13762, 94th Congress, 2d session, introduced by Representatives Bill Frenzel (R-Minn.), Barber B. Conable, Jr. (R-N.Y.), and James R. Jones (D-Okla.). Bills introduced in that Congress (1975–1976) that carried the same title as H.R. 7906 in the 91st Congress included H.R. 9 by Representative Rodino and S. 2080 by Senators Mathias and Ribicoff.

[41] See quotation from the task force report in U.S., Congress, Senate, Subcommittee on Taxation and Debt Management of the Finance Committee, *Hearings on S. 983 and S. 1688,* 96th Congress, 2d session (hereafter cited as *1980 Hearings on S. 983 and S. 1688*), pp. 689–94.

[42] Bills to regulate and foster commerce among the states by providing for the taxation of interstate commerce were as follows: S. 983 by Senator Mathias and H.R. 8277 by Representative James T. Broyhill (R-N.C.). H.R. 5076 was introduced by Representatives Conable and James R. Jones. Senators Mathias, Walter D. Huddleston (D-Ky.), and Malcolm Wallop (R-Wyo.) introduced S. 1688 in the 1st session of the 96th Congress.

[43] Property owned by the taxpayer would be valued at its original cost, and property rented by the taxpayer would be valued at eight times the net annual rental rate. Compensation, for payroll purposes, is considered as paid in the state where the employee's services are performed. Performance of some services outside the state would not change that result if services performed there were "incidental" to those performed within the state. Compensation could be considered as paid in the state in which the employee's base of operations

is located if some of the employee's service is performed in that state. If no services are performed in a state where the base of operations is located, the state from which the services are directed or controlled could count the compensation if some of the employee's services are performed there. If the services are not performed at least in part in a state in which the base of operations is located or in which the services are directed and controlled, the compensation would be counted in the state of the employee's residence. Sales of tangible personal property would be considered as effected within the state in which the purchaser, other than the U.S. government, received delivery or shipment. The "sales destination test," of course, favors market states heavily penetrated by interstate sellers from other jurisdictions. If the purchaser is the U.S. government, or the firm selling the property is not taxable in the state in which the purchaser is located, the situs of the sale would be in the state from which the property is shipped. Sales other than sales of tangible personal property would be in the state in which the income-producing activity, or a greater portion of that activity, based on cost of performance, took place.

[44] Allocation would be made to the state in which property is located in the following instances. Rents and royalties from real property would be taxable to the firm in the state in which the property is located, and those from tangible personal property would also be taxable there, to the extent the latter property is utilized in that state. Rents and royalties for tangible personal property utilized in more than one state would be allocated to those states in proportion to the number of days it was utilized in each. Capital gains and losses from the sale of real property would be taxable to the firm in the state in which the property is located. Capital gains and losses from the sale of tangible personal property would be allocated to the state in which the property was situated at the time of sale.

A firm would be taxed on nonbusiness income consisting of rents and royalties from patents and copyrights in the state in which these are utilized, to the extent they are used in that state.

A firm would be taxed on its nonbusiness income in the state of commercial domicile in the following circumstances. Interest and dividend income and gains or losses from the sale of intangible personal property would always be assigned to the state of commercial domicile. If the firm is not organized under the laws of the state in which tangible personal property is located, rents and royalties from that property would be taxed in the state of commercial domicile. If the firm is not taxable in the state in which tangible personal property is located, capital gains and losses from its sale would be taxable in the state of commercial domicile. If patents and copyrights are utilized in a state in which the firm is not taxable, or if the basis for recording royalties does not permit allocation of income to other states, or if accounting procedures do not reflect the state of utilization, these rents and royalties would be taxable in the state of the firm's commercial domicile. These provisions are included to avoid the anomaly of income that escapes taxation either because of differing state tax law provisions or because the state of preferred tax situs neglects to tax the income.

[45] Public Law 86–272 adopted in the wake of the *Northwestern States Portland Cement Company* case authorized a study to recommend legislation establishing uniform standards to be observed by the states in taxing income from interstate businesses.

[46] 434 U.S. 452 (1958). The Court majority acknowledged that a literal reading of the compact clause of the Constitution, article 1, section 10, clause 3, requires the states to obtain congressional approval before entering into such agreement among themselves, but it was reluctant to circumscribe this method of interstate cooperation since it did not "enhance state power to the detriment of federal supremacy." Justices White and Blackmun dissented from the Court's finding of validity because of the lack of congressional consent.

[47] Multistate Tax Commission Apportionment Regulation IV.1, in *State and Local Taxes (All-States Unit)* (Englewood Cliffs, N.J.: Prentice-Hall, 1977), paragraphs 631–33.

[48] Regular members of the Multistate Tax Commission include Alaska, Arkansas, California, Colorado, Hawaii, Idaho, Kansas, Michigan, Missouri, Montana, Nebraska, New Mexico, North Dakota, Oregon, South Dakota, Texas, Utah, Washington, and West Virginia. Associate members include Alabama, Arizona, Georgia, Louisiana, Maryland, Massachusetts, Minnesota, New Jersey, Ohio, Pennsylvania, and Tennessee.

[49] U.S., Congress, House of Representatives, Committee on Ways and Means, *Hearings on Income Tax Treaties,* 96th Congress, 2d session, April 29, 1980 (hereafter cited as *House Hearings on Income Tax Treaties*), pp. 61–80, statement of H. David Rosenbloom. Rosenbloom outlines in general terms the tax provisions of existing tax treaties. That the provisions of self-executing treaties control over contrary state law, see Zschernig v. Miller, 389 U.S. 429 (1962); Kolovrat v. Oregon, 366 U.S. 187 (1961); *House Hearings on Income Tax Treaties,* pp. 3, 24, statement of David H. Brockway, Joint Committee on Taxation.

[50] U.S., Congress, House of Representatives, Committee on Ways and Means, *Hearings on Tax Reform,* 94th Congress, 1st session, July 1975 (hereafter cited as *1975 Tax Reform Hearings*), p. 2032, quoting from Smith's book *Federal Tax Reform.*

[51] *Description of H.R. 5076 Relating to State Taxation of Foreign Source Corporate Income,* committee print of the Joint Committee on Taxation, March 31, 1980, p. 15. The United Kingdom treaty would benefit states and localities because of certain credit and refund provisions that advantage U.S. corporate and individual stockholders. The United Kingdom adopted a new method of integrating its corporate and individual income tax systems in 1973. Under this integrated system, United Kingdom stockholders receive with their dividends a refundable credit equal to the advance corporation tax. This credit would not be available to nonresident stockholders in the United States absent a treaty provision. That provision was expected to yield returns to U.S. investment of $381 million in retroactive payments through 1978 and annual payments of $85 million thereafter.

[52] Senator Frank Church (D-Idaho) proposed the reservation during Senate debate, but the reservation lost by a vote of 34 to 44. The administration could not then muster the two-thirds vote required to obtain ratification. The Treasury Department then acceded to the treaty reservation, and the treaty was ratified. See *Description of H.R. 5076,* pp. 15–16.

[53] See *State Tax Report No. 134* (Washington, D.C.: Committee on State Taxation of the Council of State Chambers of Commerce, October 16, 1980), pp. 1–2.

[54] The bill would exclude the following types of corporations: commercial banks, trust companies, savings banks, industrial banks, land banks, safe deposit companies, private banks, small loan companies or associations, credit unions, cooperative banks, insurance companies, and any corporations that derive 90 percent or more of their gross income from interest payments and discounts. The bill would also exclude corporations engaged in the transportation of property or passengers for hire or in rendering services incidental to such transportation, corporations engaged in the sale of electrical energy or water, or furnishing public telegraph or intrastate telephone services, if such corporations derive 50 percent or more of their ordinary gross income from such business activities.

[55] Although not defined as business or nonbusiness income, dividends from corporations in which the taxpaying firm owns less than 50 percent of the voting stock would be assigned to the state of commercial domicile and could not be apportioned to any other state. The property factor would be a fraction, the numerator of which would be the average value of corporate real property and tangible personal property owned and used or rented during the taxable years and located in the taxing state. The denominator would include the average value of such property located everywhere, but the state or the corporation could elect to exclude property from which income from foreign sources is derived. The same exclusion

could be made as to wages and sales from which foreign source income is derived in those income factors of the formula. The payroll factor would be constructed in the same manner as the property factor, and the provisions of 26 U.S.C. 303(b), 861, 862, and 863 would apply in determining the foreign source of income for the purposes of all three factors. Transactions between affiliated corporations at other than fair market value would presumably be recomputed under the arm's-length standard employed by the Internal Revenue Service. Specific ground rules affecting the application of the sales factor include the following. Sales of tangible personal property would be included in the income of the corporation for the state in which the property is ultimately received by the purchaser. Sales other than tangible property would have their situs in the state in which the income-producing activity is performed or in which a greater portion of that activity is performed, judged on the basis of the costs of performance. Sales of services would have situs in the state in which the services are performed or, if performed in more than one state, services would be divided according to the direct costs of performance incurred in each state. Sales of real property, if the corporation is engaged in the business of selling real estate, would be included in the numerator of the sales factor for the state in which the property is located. Sales that consist of the receipt of rentals from tangible personal property would be included in the numerator of the sales factor for the state in which the property is located. Gross receipts from sales other than those enumerated above would be excluded from both the numerator and the denominator of the sales factor.

[56] Corporations are "affiliated" if they are members of a group connected through stock ownership with a common owner (either corporate or noncorporate) by ownership of 50 percent or more of the voting stock of each member of one or more other members, and more than 50 percent of the voting stock of at least one of the subsidiary corporations is owned directly by the common owner.

[57] For the computation of this exclusion, see "JCT Staff Pamphlet Describing S. 983 and S. 1688 [96th Congress] on Taxation of Foreign Source Income," *Bureau of National Affairs Daily Report for Executives* (hereafter cited as *BNA DER*), June 24, 1980, pp. J–1, J–6. Also see *1980 House Hearings on State Taxation of Foreign Source Income,* p. 163, statement of Christian.

[58] The sale of motor vehicles and boats registered and motor fuels consumed in the taxing state would be excluded from these restrictions.

[59] See Advisory Commission on Intergovernmental Relations, *Significant Features of Fiscal Federalism,* p. 59; *1980 House Hearings on State Taxation of Foreign Source Income,* pp. 340–41, statement of Ferdinand P. Schoettle, University of Minnesota.

[60] Duplication in domestic taxation would, according to Lubick, be eliminated if each taxing jurisdiction used exactly the same formula. *1980 House Hearings on State Taxation of Foreign Source Income,* p. 3, statement of Lubick. Some advocates of federal legislation say that it should go beyond the changes that would be effected by the pending bills and provide clear definitions of business and nonbusiness income, and that precise rules should be spelled out for attributing various types of nonbusiness income to specific taxing jurisdictions. See "Proposals for Improvement of Interstate Taxation Bills," *Tax Lawyer,* vol. 25 (1971), pp. 443–72. Some advocates favor making the nexus requirements for state jurisdiction to tax income the same as would be provided in S. 983 for jurisdiction to impose a gross receipts tax. *Senate Hearings on Interstate Taxation,* p. 359, statement of George D. Webster, American Apparel Manufacturers Association. Other advocates argue that there should be one uniform set of rules governing jurisdiction to impose income taxes to replace varying state interpretations of Public Law 86–272.

[61] *1980 House Hearings on State Taxation of Foreign Source Income,* p. 194, statement of

Dallas A. Hurston, assistant director of taxes, the Coca-Cola Co., p. 191; statement of Thomas J. McHugh, Kraft, Inc.; and p. 183, statement of James W. McGrath, director of domestic tax law, R. J. Reynolds Industries, Inc., who contended that state rules as to when the unitary system is to be applied are vague and subjective and prone to manipulation to maximize tax revenues.

[62] Justice Powell maintained that Iowa's single-factor sales apportionment formula operated as a tariff on goods manufactured in other states and as a subsidy to Iowa manufacterers selling their goods outside Iowa in states that employed the three-factor formula. Iowa's tax, according to Justice Powell, resulted in the imposition of a tax that discriminated against interstate commerce by providing a direct commercial advantage to local business. The surcharge on Iowa sales by out-of-state businesses could be avoided only by locating all property and payroll in Iowa, and to the extent that an Iowa manufacturer made sales in other states its income tax liability to all states would be reduced, for it incurred no Iowa income tax liability on those sales. Thus, the Iowa formula penalized out-of-state manufacturers selling in Iowa and subsidized Iowa manufacturers selling in other states. 437 U.S. 283–84. Some scholars refer to this type of practice as "exporting taxes," since the tax discriminates against nonvoting out-of-state sellers. Compare Eugene F. Corrigan, "Interstate Corporate Income Taxation," *Vanderbilt Law Review*, vol. 29 (1976), pp. 423–24. See also *1980 House Hearings on State Taxation of Foreign Source Income*, p. 184, statement of McGrath.

[63] *Senate Hearings on Interstate Taxation*, p. 84, statement of John J. Mahoney, Johns-Manville Corp.; *1980 Hearings on S. 983 and S. 1688*, p. 53, statement of Donald C. Lubick, assistant secretary of the Treasury for tax policy (state differences in definition of business and nonbusiness income). Also see "Proposals for Improvement of Interstate Taxation Bills," *Tax Lawyer*, vol. 25 (1971), pp. 448–57 (state differences in the division of certain types of income and assignment of income to jurisdictions having little or no connection with the assets or activities that give rise to income).

[64] *1980 House Hearings on State Taxation of Foreign Source Income*, p. 292, statement of John S. Nolan, counsel, British National Committee of the International Chamber of Commerce and the Confederation of British Industry.

[65] Ibid., p. 213, statement of Russell Schellenberger, assistant treasurer, Foseco, Inc.

[66] Ibid., p. 167, statement of Paul W. Cook, National Association of Manufacturers; p. 183, statement of McGrath; p. 215, statement of Roger Kirk, vice chairman of the board, Brown & Williamson Tobacco Corp.; pp. 253, 255, statement of Carlyle O. Livingston for Arthur Andersen & Co.; p. 363, letter from Dennis P. Bedell, chairman, American Mining Congress Tax Committee; pp. 491, 494, statement of Valentine Brooks, attorney for Chase Brass Co.; Dallas A. Hurston, assistant director of taxes for the Coca-Cola Co., on p. 194 of the hearings, reported that in 1978 the production of a dollar of net income in the United States required more than twice the domestic sales and payroll and more than three times the domestic property needed to produce a dollar of income abroad. See also Senator Mathias, "Interstate Taxation Act of 1979," *Congressional Record*, vol. 125 (April 23, 1979), p. S 4464.

[67] *Senate Hearings on Interstate Taxation*, p. 415, statement of Dennis Amundson, deputy director, California Department of Economic and Business Development; *1980 House Hearings on State Taxation of Foreign Source Income*, p. 211; statement of Robert E. Dillon, Jr., senior vice president, finance, Sony Corporation of America; p. 205, statement of Roy A. Gentles, president of ALCAN Aluminum Corporation; p. 275, statement of G. Kenneth Christrup, director of taxes for Xerox Corporation, for the Rochester Tax Council; p. 271, statement of Lyle Bethune, assistant controller and director of taxes, Anderson, Clayton &

Company; p. 169, statement of Cook, National Association of Manufacturers (Cook's statement challenges the claim of proponents of worldwide combination that this approach has the merit of uniformity); pp. 160–61, statement of Christian; p. 255, statement of Livingston.

[68] *1980 House Hearings on State Taxation of Foreign Source Income,* p. 161, statement of Christian; pp. 124–25, statement of Representative Conable; p. 171, statement of Cook; p. 185, statement of James R. Pratt, vice president and director of taxes, General Mills, Inc.; p. 386, letter from P. H. Friedman, vice president for taxes, Pfizer, Inc.; *Senate Hearings on Interstate Taxation,* p. 79, statement of Richard C. Tveter, manager, state and local taxes, International Mineral and Chemical Company.

[69] *Senate Hearings on Interstate Taxation,* p. 115, statement of James D. Whisenhand, deputy attorney general of Florida; p. 449, statement of Sterling Gallagher, commissioner of revenue for Alaska.

[70] Ibid., p. 296, statement of Donald H. Clark, commissioner of revenue for Indiana, who estimated Indiana's 1978 income tax revenues from the throwback of sales at 5 to 7 percent of its total income tax revenues, or $10 million; p. 56, statement of William Barnes, chief of the sales and income tax division of the Mississippi State Tax Commission; p. 323, statement of Wayne Golomb, deputy director, legal and investigative bureau for the Illinois Department of Revenue, who maintained that omitting a throwback provision for sales from the bill would make states that do not impose an income tax attractive as tax havens.

[71] *Senate Hearings on Interstate Taxation,* pp. 58–59, statement of Michael Norton, legal assistant to the commissioner of revenue for Tennessee.

[72] The various estimates of revenue loss in *Senate Hearings on Interstate Taxation* included Florida, $11.6 million (change in three-factor apportionment formula for income taxes); Indiana, $23 million overall; Utah, $15 million overall; South Carolina, $15 to $20 million overall; Ohio, $25 to $30 million overall; Minnesota, $56 million overall; and California, $485 million (bank and corporate income taxes). The state tax commissioner for Virginia said that Virginia would not lose as much in revenues as was lost when the federal government adopted the asset depreciation range, but he did not provide an overall loss figure.

[73] States that do not have a corporate income tax are Michigan, Nevada, South Dakota, Texas, Washington, and Wyoming.

[74] "Accounting: Treasury, Businesses Support Bills Barring States' Use of Unitary Method," *BNA DER,* June 24, 1980, pp. G–4, G–6.

[75] *Senate Hearings on Interstate Taxation,* pp. 781–82.

[76] House Report 1480, 88th Congress, 2d session.

[77] In *Senate Hearings on Interstate Taxation,* p. 265, Donald K. Barnes, special counsel for Moorman Manufacturing Company, in his prepared statement contended:

> Complaints by state officials that the bill would reduce their income are completely unjustified. There is no such thing as a "market state" as distinguished from a "producer state." Every state is both market and producer in equal amounts. My state of Florida is a "market" for automobiles. How does it pay for them? Not in money, because Florida doesn't print money. It pays with oranges and resort hotels. Thus, if Florida taxes all the income of orange groves and the hotel proprietors, it gets all it has coming to it without taxing the out-of-state activities of the automobile factories. There is no more reason for Florida to collect a tax—as the sales factor does—on Michigan factories than for Michigan to collect a tax on Florida hotel rooms occupied by Michigan residents—who are the "market."

[78] See, for example, *1980 House Hearings on State Taxation of Foreign Source Income,* p. 164, statement of Christian; pp. 292–93, statement of Nolan quoting Laurence C. Woodworth, assistant secretary of the Treasury.

[79] See, for example, *Senate Hearings on Interstate Taxation,* p. 105, statement of Thomas R. Moor, manager of state and local taxes, Akzona, Inc.

[80] Moorman Manufacturing Co. v. Bair, 437 U.S. 267, 279 (1978).

[81] See, for example, *Senate Hearings on Interstate Taxation,* pp. 415–16, statement of Amundson.

[82] *Congressional Record,* vol. 127 (March 10, 1980), p. S 1982. As to the egregious nature of including the income of foreign parent corporations of a U.S. subsidiary, see *1980 House Hearings on State Taxation of Foreign Source Income,* p. 295, statement of Nolan.

[83] *1980 House Hearings on State Taxation of Foreign Source Income,* pp. 154–64, statement of Christian; p. 281, letter from the Rochester Tax Council; p. 147, statement of Charles W. Wheeler, senior tax attorney, Chamber of Commerce of the United States. The tax section of the New York State Bar has cited the taxation of intercorporate dividends as a particularly troublesome problem that is exacerbated when the corporations involved are under common ownership. The taxation of dividends paid by a subsidiary to a parent corporation, according to the tax section, subjects a single economic gain to duplicative taxation and discriminates against businesses that find it impractical to operate other than in a multicorporate form (particularly when they operate in foreign countries) by requiring them to bear a disproportionate share of the tax burden. Senator Mathias, "Reporting State Tax Liability," p. S 301.

[84] *Senate Hearings on Interstate Taxation,* p. 351.

[85] *1980 House Hearings on State Taxation of Foreign Source Income,* p. 355.

[86] "Accounting: Treasury, Businesses Support Bills Barring States' Use of Unitary Method," *BNA DER,* p. G–6, statement of Reuben Johnson, director of legislative services for the National Farmers Union. Also see *1980 House Hearings on State Taxation of Foreign Source Income,* pp. 36, 123, 125, statement of Theodore W. de Looze, chief tax counsel, Oregon Department of Justice; pp. 131–32, statements of James W. Hamilton, California State Franchise Tax Board, and Harriet A. King, commissioner, Vermont Department of Taxes.

[87] *1980 House Hearings on State Taxation of Foreign Source Income,* p. 37.

[88] Ibid., pp. 69–89, position paper of the California State Franchise Tax Board. Opponents cite *Summary of International Cases Involving Section 482 of the Internal Revenue Code* (Washington, D.C.: Treasury Department, January 8, 1973), which concludes that the arm's-length method failed to account accurately for taxable income in 40 percent of the instances in which it was used to make adjustments. A study by Jane O. Burns, "How the I.R.S. Applies the Intercompany Pricing Rules of Section 482: A Corporate Survey," *Journal of Taxation,* vol. 54 (May 1980), estimated that there was double taxation of corporate income in 52 percent of the cases in which the IRS employed the arm's-length method.

[89] *1980 House Hearings on State Taxation of Foreign Source Income,* p. 325, statement of Jonathan Rowe, Citizens for Tax Justice; p. 36, statement of de Looze.

[90] Memorandum from executive director of the Advisory Commission on Intergovernmental Relations, March 26, 1981, attachment cited as Back-Up Chapters, pp. 1–2, 36.

[91] *Senate Hearings on Interstate Taxation,* p. 36, statement of de Looze. On p. 35 of the hearings, Kenneth Cory, state controller for the California State Franchise Tax Board,

estimated in 1980 that legislation then being considered by the California legislature to limit the application of the unitary business principle as to foreign parent corporations would cost the state $35 million in revenues annually. However, Amundson of the California Department of Economic and Business Development estimated the revenue loss at a more conservative $6 to $8 million. See *Senate Hearings on Interstate Taxation,* p. 415.

[92] *Senate Hearings on Interstate Taxation,* pp. 483–88, statement of Franklin C. Latcham; *1980 House Hearings on State Taxation of Foreign Source Income,* p. 356, statement of Nolan; p. 152, statement of Edward L. Hennessy, Jr., chairman of the board and chief executive officer of Allied Chemical Corporation, for the Business Roundtable. Latcham says that the unitary method is based on the following erroneous assumptions when applied to multinational corporations: (1) that all corporate members of a unitary group are operating in a common market where wages, prices, and costs of tangible property are about the same and where there are no substantial long-standing differences in economic, political, and social conditions; (2) that a dollar of wages or sales or a dollar invested in tangible property will earn about the same income by all corporations that are members of the unitary group; and (3) that neither the companies nor the taxing authorities can determine the separate profits earned by each member of the unitary group nor appropriate arm's-length pricing for intercompany transactions.

[93] *Senate Hearings on Interstate Taxation,* pp. 126–28, 137–38, statement of Marchese; p. 145, statement of Richard Tryon, president, Colwell Company; p. 219, statement of William F. Harlton, Jr., vice president, Detroit Veterinary Supply Company; pp. 270–71, statement of Prentice Cushing, Jr., president, G. K. Heller Corporation; p. 95, statement of David Stump, president, Jackson & Perkins Company; p. 65, statement of Senator Mathias; p. 199, statement of John D. Naughton, manager of state taxes for Republic Steel Corporation; p. 251, statement of Wayne A. Scheider, director of tax administration, Owens-Corning Fiberglas Corporation.

[94] Ibid., pp. 373–74, statement of Corrigan.

[95] Ibid., p. 60, statement of S. J. Owens, director of the sales and use tax division, Tennessee Department of Revenue; p. 182, statement of William R. Cave, assistant executive director, Florida Department of Revenue; p. 328, statement of David C. Hardesty, Jr., tax commissioner for West Virginia; p. 301, statement of Golomb; p. 372, statement of Sarah Bennett for New Mexico; p. 54, statement of Barnes; p. 164, statement of Robert Wasson, chairman, South Carolina Tax Commission. Also see *Senate Hearings on S. 983 and S. 1688,* p. 969, statement of New York State Department of Taxation and Finance.

[96] *Senate Hearings on Interstate Taxation,* pp. 54–55, statement of Barnes; pp. 114, 121, statement of Whisenhand; p. 307, statement of Benjamin C. Holderied, Michigan State Department of the Treasury; p. 155, statement of Wasson; p. 291, statement of Edgar L. Lindley, commissioner, Ohio Department of Taxation; p. 294, statement of Clark; p. 366, statement of Martin Huff, National Association of Tax Administrators; pp. 369–70, statement of Douglas D. Bell, executive secretary, California State Board of Equalization.

[97] Ibid., p. 291, statement of Lindley; pp. 295–96, statement of Clark; p. 301, statement of Golomb; p. 372, statement of Bennett.

[98] *Senate Hearings on S. 983 and S. 1688,* pp. 257–58.

[99] *Senate Hearings on Interstate Taxation,* pp. 72–74, statement of Tveter; p. 359, statement of Webster.

[100] Ibid., pp. 202–3, statement of Naughton; p. 249, statement of Scheider; pp. 358–59, statement of Webster. Some advocates would extend the restrictions of S. 983 to the im-

position of gross receipts taxes on intangibles. New Mexico, for example, considers use of a franchiser's trademark in that state as a sufficient connection with the state to justify its imposition of a gross receipts tax on all royalties and other payments received from a franchise holder in that state. See p. 245, statement of Paul H. Coleman, vice president and corporate counsel, Arthur Treacher's Fish and Chips, Inc. One opponent of the legislation objected to the bill because it does not address the problem of taxing income from leases, service contracts, intangibles, and so forth. See p. 296, statement of Lindley.

[101] Ibid., p. 295, statement of Clark; p. 326, statement of Hardesty; p. 368, statement of Martin. Also see *Senate Hearings on S.983 and S.1688,* p. 412, statement of William D. Dexter, general counsel of the Multistate Tax Commission.

[102] *1980 House Hearings on State Taxation of Foreign Source Income,* pp. 169–70, statement of Cook; *Senate Hearings on S.983 and S.1688,* p. 40, statement of Lubick.

[103] *1980 House Hearings on State Taxation of Foreign Source Income,* pp. 165, 170, statement of Cook; pp. 253, 255, statement of Livingston. Also see *Senate Hearings on Interstate Taxation,* pp. 491, 494, statement of Brooks.

[104] *1980 House Hearings on State Taxation of Foreign Source Income,* p. 700.

[105] Ibid., pp. 170–71, statement of Cook; p. 173, statement of James M. Bodfish, president of the Tax Executives Institute, Inc.; p. 191, statement of McHugh; p. 214, statement of Schellenberger. Also see *Senate Hearings on Interstate Taxation,* p. 78, statement of Bethune; p. 206, statement of Stanley D. Fraser, vice president for taxes for St. Joe Paper Company; p. 494, statement of Brooks.

[106] *Senate Hearings on Interstate Taxation,* p. 258, statement of R. Donald Bell, vice president and controller of the Ball Corporation; p. 488, statement of Latcham. Also see *1980 House Hearings on State Taxation of Foreign Source Income,* p. 146, statement of Wheeler.

[107] *Senate Hearings on Interstate Taxation,* p. 87, statement of Stump; p. 127, statement of Marchese; p. 222, statement of Glenn Wonderly, Perfection Photo Company. Also see *1980 House Hearings on State Taxation of Foreign Source Income,* p. 136, statement of Senator Mathias.

[108] *Senate Hearings on Interstate Taxation,* pp. 244–45, statement of William C. Becker, controller, Paramount International Coin Corporation.

[109] Ibid., pp. 127, 132–34, statement of Marchese.

[110] Ibid., p. 158, statement of Wasson; p. 452, statement of Steve Smith, president of the California Tax Reform Association; pp. 462–63, statement of Alan Charnes, executive director of the Colorado Department of Revenue. The chief tax counsel for the Oregon Department of Justice believes that the burdens of the two competing systems of accounting for income are probably about equal. See *1980 House Hearings on State Taxation of Foreign Source Income,* p. 37, statement of de Looze. Also see "Proposals for Improvement," *Tax Lawyer,* p. 448.

[111] *Senate Hearings on S. 983 and S. 1688,* p. 49, statement of Lubick.

[112] *Senate Hearings on Interstate Taxation,* pp. 114–15, statement of Whisenhand; pp. 155–56, statement of Wasson; p. 190, statement of W. W. Forst, state tax commissioner, commonwealth of Virginia.

[113] *Senate Hearings on Interstate Taxation,* p. 116, statement of Whisenhand; p. 174, statement of Brooks; p. 156, statement of Wasson; p. 334, statement of Golomb.

[114] Ibid., pp. 486–88, statement of Latcham; *1980 House Hearings on State Taxation of Foreign Source Income,* p. 171, statement of Cook.

[115] *Congressional Record,* vol. 125 (April 23, 1979), p. S 4464, statement of Senator Mathias; *Congressional Record,* vol. 126 (October 2, 1980), p. E 4745, statement of Representative Broyhill; *Senate Hearings on Interstate Taxation,* p. 219, statement of Harlton; p. 227, statement of Thomas B. Kyle, Jr., vice president, operations, Spring Hill Nurseries. Also see "Accounting: Treasury, Businesses Support Bills Barring States' Use of Unitary Method," *BNA DER,* p. G–5.

[116] *Regional Growth: Interstate Tax Competition* (Washington, D.C.: Advisory Commission on Intergovermental Relations, 1981), pp. 4–5, 15, 26, 32–51, 68–72. Also see "A Counterattack in the War between the States," *Business Week,* June 21, 1976, p. 71. In *Senate Hearings on Interstate Taxation,* p. 452, Steve Smith cites an M.I.T. study showing that neither comparative long-term growth trends nor surveys of business opinion indicate that tax differentials among states are major factors in location decisions. The Industrial States Policy Center estimates that California's use of the unitary method with worldwide combination accounting accounts for only 6.25 percent of that state's business taxes and would raise a corporation's costs of locating in that state by only 0.1875 percent. *Senate Hearings on Interstate Taxation,* p. 864.

[117] Senator Mathias cites examples of multinational corporations that refused to establish plants or business locations in California because of its broad application of the unitary business principle and worldwide combination accounting. *Senate Hearings on S. 983 and S. 1688,* p. 63. Also see pp. 68–71, excerpts from California Assembly Committee on Revenue and Taxation committee hearings; p. 81, statement of Donald J. Kapraly, ALCAN Aluminum Corporation. Schoettle uses the illustration of the hypothetical state with an 8 percent marginal tax rate on corporate income. If the state's application of its apportionment formula permits it in effect to tax an equal amount of out-of-state income, the corporation's post-tax return will be reduced by 8.7 percent, a change nearly as large as that produced by the federal investment tax credit, which is thought by many to influence corporate business decisions (see *Senate Hearings on S. 983 and S. 1688,* p. 819). Lubick recommended that Congress ban the use of the unitary principle for foreign parent corporations. He said a ban on use of the unitary principle would not be inappropriate for U.S. multinationals, although he did prefer additional study before effecting that change. Ibid., p. 40. Also see *1980 House Hearings on State Taxation of Foreign Source Income,* pp. 6–7.

[118] *1980 House Hearings on State Taxation of Foreign Source Income,* p. 138; p. 340, statement of Schoettle as to the need for a coherent tax policy.

[119] Senator Mathias, "Reporting State Tax Liability," p. S 302.

[120] *1980 House Hearings on State Taxation of Foreign Source Income,* p. 380, statement of International Business Machine Corporation.

[121] Norman B. Ture, "Taxing Foreign-Source Income," in *U.S. Taxation of American Business Abroad* (Washington, D.C.: American Enterprise Institute–Hoover Institution on War, Revolution and Peace, 1975), pp. 37, 64–66. Ture cites the example of an American corporation providing capital to a foreign subsidiary corporation that imports machine tools from the United States. The production of machine tools in the United States imposes real costs in this country, but the income payments on account of that production are already taxed here, and once the machine tools are in place abroad they impose no additional costs in this country. Ture notes that the fact that the foreign company is a subsidiary of a U.S. firm does not convert the foreign subsidiary's income into U.S. income.

[122] See, for example, Dan Throop Smith, "Issues in U.S. Taxation of Business Investment Abroad," in *U.S. Taxation,* pp. 83, 88.

[123] *1980 House Hearings on State Taxation of Foreign Source Income,* p. 302, statement of Nolan; p. 390, statement of Price, Waterhouse and Company. Also see *Congressional Record,* vol. 127 (March 10, 1981), p. S 1983, statement of Senator Mathias. Also see *Senate Hearings on Interstate Taxation,* p. 128, statement of Marchese.

[124] Assembly Bill 525, which passed the California Assembly in 1980 but failed in conference, would have amended California law to provide that in determining the income of a business entity the state would not take into consideration the income and apportionment factors of any other business entity that was created or organized under the laws of a foreign country, that was not owned and controlled by a U.S. corporation or by residents of the United States, and that had more than 50 percent of its operations outside the United States, its political territories and possessions, and the Commonwealth of Puerto Rico. This would have effectively excluded the income factors of foreign parent corporations, for example, from worldwide combination accounting for affected unitary businesses. Certain types of business activities, energy, steel, and agriculture would have been exempted from the provisions of the bill. See *Senate Hearings on Interstate Taxation,* p. 308, statement of Nolan; p. 346, statement of J. Robert Vastine, chairman of the legislative committee for the California Council for International Trade. Had this legislation been enacted, it would have represented a major shift away from worldwide combination accounting for the income of unitary operations of affiliated firms employed in California and certain other states that are members of the Multistate Tax Compact.

[125] *Congressional Record,* vol. 127 (February 23, 1981), p. E 620; statement of Representative Conable. Also see *Congressional Record,* vol. 125 (April 23, 1979), p. S 4465, statement of Senator Mathias. Also see *1980 House Hearings on State Taxation of Foreign Source Income,* p. 138, statement of Senator Mathias; p. 158, statement of Christian; p. 172, statement of Cook; p. 205, statement of Gentles; p. 275, statement of Christrup. Compare Dan Throop Smith in *U.S. Taxation,* p. 93. He argues that federal taxation of income from foreign sources at the full corporate tax rate, by abolishing the foreign tax credit, would substantially reduce federal revenues, even though these might increase initially.

[126] Wilson E. Schmidt, "U.S. Capital Export Policy; Backdoor Mercantilism," in *U.S. Taxation,* pp. 7, 13–14, 17. Also see Oswald W. Brownlee, *Taxing the Income from U.S. Corporation Investments Abroad* (Washington, D.C.: American Enterprise Institute, 1979), p. 19, and Lawrence B. Krause and Kenneth W. Dam, *Federal Tax Treatment of Foreign Income* (Washington, D.C.: Brookings Institution, 1964), p. 46.

[127] See the discussion of these changes effected by the Revenue Act of 1962 in Krause and Dam, *Federal Tax Treatment,* pp. 33–41.

[128] G. C. Hufbauer, "A Guide to Law and Policy," in *U.S. Taxation,* pp. 1, 4.

[129] *Congressional Record,* vol. 119 (January 4, 1973), p. S 151. Representative James A. Burke (D-Mass.) reintroduced this bill as H.R. 63 in the 92d Congress, 1st session, and Senator Vance Hartke (D-Ind.) reintroduced it as S. 151 in that Congress.

[130] *Senate Hearings on S. 983 and S. 1688,* p. 48.

[131] "Accounting: Treasury, Businesses Support Bills Barring States' Use of Unitary Method," *BNA DER,* p. G–5, statement of Rueben Johnson, National Farmers Union.

[132] *Senate Hearings on S. 983 and S. 1688,* p. 363, statement of Senator Church. Also see Schmidt, in *U.S. Taxation,* pp. 13–14.

[133] See Brownlee, *Taxing the Income,* p. 16, for the percentage of U.S. direct investment abroad devoted to manufacturing in 1977.

[134] The ratio of effective tax to income in 1977 of a typical U.S. manufacturing corporation with no income from foreign sources is estimated at 37 to 38 percent, while the effective U.S. tax rate paid by American firms on foreign investments ranges from 27.5 percent to 47.5 percent, and one scholar estimates that such rates sometimes exceed 58 percent. The average overall U.S. tax rate on the foreign manufacturing subsidiaries of U.S. corporations is estimated at about 40 percent. Brownlee, *Taxing the Income,* pp. 3, 19; see also Krause and Dam, *Federal Tax Treatment,* pp. 50–51; and Schmidt, in *U.S. Taxation,* p. 16. Also see *1980 House Hearings on Taxation of Foreign Source Income,* p. 201, statement of McHugh.

[135] See Ture, in *U.S. Taxation,* pp. 39, 63–66. The usual alternative definitions of tax neutrality are that tax arrangements are neutral if they result in an allocation of capital among nations that maximizes worldwide income and product, or that tax arrangements are neutral if they result in the allocation of capital that maximizes the home jurisdiction's product and income. See Krause and Dam, *Federal Tax Treatment,* p. 28, on the history of tax law changes.

[136] Hufbauer, in *U.S. Taxation,* pp. 4–6; Brownlee, *Taxing Income,* p. 6.

[137] See Ture, in *U.S. Taxation,* pp. 46 and 60; Smith, in *U.S. Taxation,* p. 90. Even if government policy restricted foreign direct investment by U.S. firms, proponents contend that this would not necessarily mean increased investment domestically, since money will usually seek its highest rate of return. Thus, it would probably flow back overseas, through banking channels for example. Brownlee notes that if U.S. investment were made larger at the expense of investment in the rest of the world through additional adjustments in tax policy, the rate of return on capital investment in the United States would fall and the rate of return on overseas investment would rise. See Brownlee, *Taxing Income,* p. 21, and *Survey of Current Business* (Washington, D.C.: U.S. Department of Commerce, December 1980), table 1, p. 50, lines 12 and 49.

[138] Ture, in *U.S. Taxation,* pp. 59–60; Smith, in *U.S. Taxation,* p. 89. Also see Timothy W. Stanley, "Why Labor Is Wrong on Multinationals," *Sigma,* no. 1 (1972), pp. 26, 28–30.

[139] Milton Friedman, "Do Imports Cost Jobs?" *Newsweek,* vol. 97 (February 9, 1981), p. 77; Smith, in *U.S. Taxation,* pp. 88–90. Smith contends that, on balance, this international division of labor increases productivity in all countries.

[140] *1980 House Hearings on State Taxation of Foreign Source Income,* p. 282, letter of William C. Penick, managing director, tax policy, Arthur Andersen & Company; p. 151, statement of Hennessy. Smith, in *U.S. Taxation,* 92, maintains that much investment by foreign subsidiaries of U.S. companies is financed locally or from old dollar holdings, and that this does not affect the balance of payments. If the foreign tax is higher than the U.S. tax, there is no incentive to delay repatriation. Schmidt, in *U.S. Taxation,* p. 17.

[141] *Survey of Current Business* (Washington, D.C.: U.S. Department of Commerce, August 1974), part II, table 2, p. 27, and explanation at p. 39.

[142] *1980 House Hearings on State Taxation of Foreign Source Income,* p. 48.

[143] Ibid., p. 48; p. 46, statement of King. Also see *Senate Hearings on Interstate Taxation,* pp. 116–17, statement of Whisenhand; p. 187, statement of Forst (when you take away state taxing authority, all you have left is a state flag, a state bird, and a state song).

[144] *Senate Hearings on S. 983 and S. 1688,* p. 359, statement of Arthur C. Roemer, president,

National Association of Tax Administrators. Other state efforts to ease the burden on multistate corporations include provisions by many states for exemption and resale certificates, omission of taxpayer charges for out-of-state audits, and extended filing periods for out-of-state sellers with minimal contacts with the taxing jurisdiction.

[145] *Eleventh Annual Report* (Denver, Colo.: Multistate Tax Commission, May 1979).

[146] Jerome R. Hellerstern, "State Taxation under the Commerce Clause," *Vanderbilt Law Review,* vol. 29 (March 1976), p. 342; *1980 House Hearings on State Taxation of Foreign Source Income,* p. 123, statement of de Looze. The joint audit program is said to recover $23 for every dollar contributed to the program by the member states.

[147] Cahoon and Brown, "The Interstate Tax Dilemma," pp. 189–90, 197; "Proposals for Improvement," *Tax Lawyer,* p. 435. Also see *Senate Hearings on Interstate Taxation,* p. 248, statement of Scheider.

[148] *Senate Hearings on Interstate Taxation*, p. 212, statement of Fraser; p. 79, statement of Bethune.

[149] Cahoon and Brown, "The Interstate Tax Dilemma," pp. 187, 189–90. Also see *Congressional Record,* vol. 125 (April 23, 1979), p. S 4464.

[150] *1980 House Hearings on State Taxation of Foreign Source Income,* p. 100, statement of Wheeler; p. 5, statement of Lubick; p. 151, statement of Hennessey; p. 158, statement of Christian; p. 186, statement of Ronald J. Joranko, director of taxes, TRW, Inc.; p. 274, statement of Christrup; p. 283, statement of Nolan. Also see *Senate Hearings on Interstate Taxation,* p. 483, statement of Latcham; p. 495, statement of Brooks. Also see *Congressional Record,* vol. 115 (February 4, 1969), p. S 2597, statement of Senator Ribicoff. Also see "State Taxes: Conable, Jones Reintroduce Bill on States' Use of Unitary Accounting Method," *BNA DER,* March 2, 1981, p. G–1.

[151] *Senate Hearings on S. 983 and S. 1688,* p. 45. See also "Tax Treaties: Major Issues on New Income Tax Treaties with Belgium, Austria Discussed at Treasury Hearings," *BNA DER,* March 24, 1981, pp. G–9, G–10 (Belgium wants an end to the unitary method of income taxation).

[152] Senate Report 658, 68th Congress, 1st session, pp. 10–14, views of Senators Albert Gore (D-Tenn.), Eugene McCarthy (D-Minn.), and Russell B. Long (D-La.).